MEXICO: A MIDDLE CLASS SOCIETY

Poor **No More**, Developed **Not Yet**

January 2012

Spanish edition: September 2010, Mexico, CIDAC

Mexico Institute
Woodrow Wilson Center for Scholars
One Woodrow Wilson Plaza
1300 Pennsylvania Avenue NW
Washington, DC 20004'3027
www.wilsoncenter.org/mexico

Centro de Investigación para el Desarollo, A.C.
Jaime Balmes No. 11 Edificio D, 2o piso
Col. Los Morales Polanco, 11510 México, D.F.
www.cidac.org

Design and layout: e:de, business by design
Translation: Cara Goodman

ISBN:1-933549-75-0

Printed in the United States of America

MEXICO: A MIDDLE CLASS SOCIETY

Poor **No More**, Developed **Not Yet**

LUIS DE LA CALLE
LUIS RUBIO

CIDAC

Woodrow Wilson International Center for Scholars
Mexico Institute

The Woodrow Wilson International Center for Scholars, established by Congress in 1968 and headquartered in Washington, D.C., is a living national memorial to President Wilson. The Center's mission is to commemorate the ideals and concerns of Woodrow Wilson by providing a link between the worlds of ideas and policy, while fostering research, study, discussion, and collaboration among a broad spectrum of individuals concerned with policy and scholarship in national and international affairs. Supported by public and private funds, the Center is a nonpartisan institution engaged in the study of national and world affairs. It establishes and maintains a neutral forum for free, open, and informed dialogue. Conclusions or opinions expressed in Center publications and programs are those of the authors and speakers and do not necessarily reflect the views of the Center staff, fellows, trustees, advisory groups, or any individuals or organizations that provide financial support to the Center.

The Center is the publisher of The Wilson Quarterly and home of Woodrow Wilson Center Press, dialogue radio and television. For more information about the Center's activities and publications, please visit us on the web at www.wilsoncenter.org.

Our heartfelt thanks to Manuel Aragonés and María Cristina Capelo for their work and support in this project, to Chris Wilson for coordinating it at The Wilson Center, to Andrew Selee for giving us this opportunity and to The Wilson Center for International Scholars for being such a gracious host.

Contents

Preface to the English edition

Americans may fathom the middle class as being the obvious foundation of civilization and economic development, but most Mexicans have historically seen their country as mostly poor. Unlike American politicians that attempt to appeal to the average citizen in Peoria as the epitome of the modern American, Mexican politicians tend to look at Mexican peasants in Tinguindin in the state of Michoacan or squatter towns like Chalco, in the outskirts of Mexico City. Even thinking about Mexico as a middle class society seems odd, out of place and, of course, politically incorrect. Venturing to write that Mexico is now mostly a middle class country has been deemed a provocation by some analysts and politicians accustomed to crafting their public discourse in terms of an extended and impossible to overcome poverty.

This book was born out of a rather subtle observation during the last presidential election in 2006, when Felipe Calderon won largely because he understood what his contender, Andres Manuel Lopez Obrador, did not: that Mexico was rapidly becoming a majority middle class nation.

Becoming a middle class nation entails a radical paradigm shift. It changes the way Mexicans think of themselves and it forces everyone to approach issues differently, starting with the politicians. Needless to say, not everybody agrees with the arguments presented here. Our aim in writing this book, and in the way it is written, was to signal the change and explain some of the driving forces behind it. The reader will find many caveats in the argument, but we believe that the thrust is right on target. The book does not dismiss the presence of widespread poverty, but underlines the fact that most Mexicans can no longer be considered poor (a recent development). The country is therefore better, but not yet well.

After the book was first published in Mexico, three studies came out that largely confirm our findings. One, by the Economic Commission for Latin America and the Caribbean, shows how the middle class has expanded across the board. Another one, by the Brookings Institution, compares Latin America to other regions of the world, highlighting the area's impressive advances. The Brookings study defines the middle class as those that earn enough to be above the poverty line, an approach that is similar to ours.

Mexico's 2010 Census results, published earlier this year and taking into account the severe recession of 2008-09, also largely confirm the trends we found through other indicators over the past several years.

We hope this book contributes to a better understanding of Mexico and to an appreciation of the complex nature of the country's gradual transformation in all realms of life.

Finally, we cannot be grateful enough to Andrew Selee at the Mexico Institute of the Woodrow Wilson International Center for Scholars for his interest and kindness in publishing the English version of this book.

Luis de la Calle
Luis Rubio

* * *

CIDAC (Centro de Investigación para el Desarrollo, A.C.) is an independent, not-for-profit think tank that undertakes research and proposes viable policy alternatives for the medium and long-term development of Mexico. By providing public policy proposals, analyses, and information, CIDAC seeks to contribute to strengthening the Rule of Law, creating conditions favorable to Mexico's economic and social development, and enrich Mexican public opinion.

The board of CIDAC is responsible for supervising the administration of the Center and approving its general areas of study. Nonetheless, the conclusions of its studies, as well as its publications, are the sole responsibility of the institute's professional staff.

Verónica Baz
General Director
CIDAC

What is the middle class?

Chapter 1

Social classes are generally defined according to criteria such as property, wealth, education, occupation, or social origin. Some economic theories address social class as a function of the place each person occupies in the production process, and assign philosophical values and political positions to the members of each class. Some societies revolve around class differences, just as other societies ignore their very existence. Some build political and partisan organizations around social classes, while others design mechanisms to deliberately cross the social lines that divide them. For example, in England, the Labour and Conservative parties each originally organized around a social class, whereas in the United States, the Republican and Democratic parties are not directly linked with social strata, but instead are divided by cultural and regional differences.

The concept of middle class is hard to establish and complex to grasp, but that makes it no less real nor politically relevant. From a Marxist perspective, which ties the definition of social class to the productive process (owners of the means of production versus workers), the notion of "middle class" is to a large extent repugnant. Even so, the middle classes of practically all modern societies, and all developed ones, share a common characteristic: those who are part of the middle class earn enough income to live in an urban environment and want to systematically improve their social and economic standing.

At least in a colloquial sense, the definition of a middle class person is related to some level of economic independence, even if one has little individual political or social influence. The concept of middle class is elastic because it includes people with very distinct income levels. The term encompasses professionals, business people, bureaucrats, academics, and other workers—all of whom have sufficient income to live.

A middle-class household in Mexico is generally a family living in an urban context, although there is no reason to exclude the possibility that households in rural areas are also heading in this direction. The transformation from a mostly rural and mostly poor country to a less poor, mostly middle class country occurred, in large part, thanks to the communications revolution, improved transportation, and the benefits of emigration, including remittances.

Besides the availability of sufficient incomes, the Mexican middle class is defined by a search for social mobility and advancement; employment normally within the service sector; interest in culture, film, and other artistic expressions as means of entertainment; the rental or ownership of a house or apartment for one's family; adding a second story to one's house; car ownership; or the meeting of other material needs. The same is true for owning a television, having Internet access, and participating in virtual social networks. In fact, the extent to which a country progresses in the information age, where technology and creative capacity play a fundamental role in promoting development, largely determines the kind of growth and employment opportunities that an ever-increasing number of middle class people can access.

The definition of the middle class also includes a positive worldview, an interest in enjoying life beyond the day-to-day, an expectation of systematic economic advancement, and a belief that education is essential to the development of one's children.[1]

The search for better schools is a clear demonstration of the values that motivate the middle class, and explains the remarkable growth of low or no-cost educational centers to meet this demand in Mexico. To the extent that parents associate education with success in life, the seeds of a permanent middle class are sown and a path toward systematic progress is established. To satisfy this demand, in the face of bottlenecks in the expansion of public school systems, the number of private establishments dedicated to educational services has grown from 33,495 according to INEGI's 1999 Economic Census, to 44,780 in 2009—representing an increase of 34%.

The number of people employed in the provision on these services increased by 81%, growing from 362,015 to 653,736 people. The expansion

The concept of middle class is elastic because it includes people with very distinct income levels

[1] In highly developed nations, the observation has been made that middle classes can become conformist and even pessimistic. This phenomenon may be related to a fear of losing privileges or the status quo. The way in which this phenomenon plays out in Mexico is addressed later in the book.

of private education is a widespread phenomenon, often occurring in what appear to be non-middle class communities. This expansion has taken place even as, for demographic reasons, the number of young students is declining. In sum, the combination of more personnel and less students should result in a gradual increase in the quality of education.

It can be difficult to pinpoint some of the factors that characterize the middle class; it is less complicated, however, to identify people who can be characterized by those factors in terms of politics or consumption.

To market analysts, for whom what's important is differentiating social groups according to parameters typically related to their capacity to consume, the middle class can be clearly delineated and subdivided according to income and consumption patterns. The same is true for pollsters researching electoral questions: for them, knowing someone's precise income is irrelevant—they seek instead to identify social groups according to their attitudes and profiles. Difficult though it may be to define the middle class in conceptual terms, Mexico's middle class does exist in practical terms: it is visible, and it can be measured.

MARKETING TO THE MIDDLE CLASS

Marketers have developed a scale for differentiating their target audiences according to socioeconomic characteristics and spending capacities. Their objective is to identify the correct type of advertising or communication strategy to reach potential buyers. This same scale, however, allows us to look at the composition of Mexico's population according to the same parameters.

According to the classifications developed by AMAI, a Mexican association of companies dedicated to market research and public opinion, the country's population is divided into five segments: AB (people with high purchasing power and income), C+ (people with higher-than-average incomes, whose families are headed by someone with a college degree and have at least two cars), C (people with middle incomes, whose families are headed by someone with a high school degree and have both a car and the ability to take one trip per year), D+ (people with incomes slightly below average, some secondary education and no family vehicle), D (people with low income levels and a fairly austere way of existence, who have a primary school education and who lack access to traditional banking services)

Given the generic and elastic characterizations of the middle class, these categories are useful in pinpointing its dimensions. According to AMAI's data, which in turn uses the Income-Expenditure Survey published by INEGI, Mexico's urban populations (populations of cities with more than 50,000 inhabitants) are thus distributed:

Pesos? Dlls? Per Month? Per Year? Per Family?

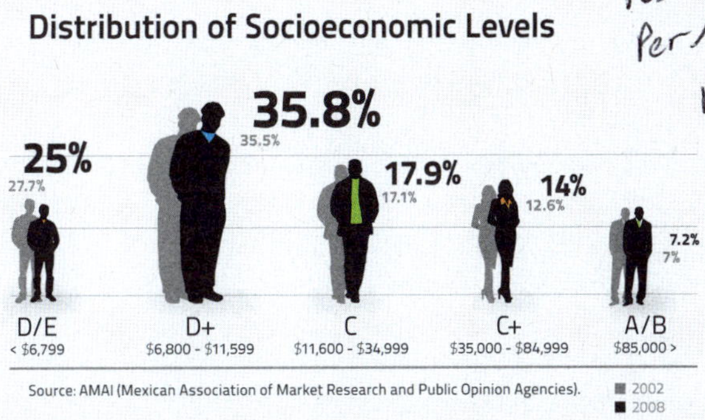

Consistent with the parameters that have thus far been discussed, the middle class would find itself at least in the D+ to C range. According to this breakdown, 53.2% of Mexico's urban population had already achieved middle-class status in 2002. This number rises if one includes some portion of the C+ population, which in many ways is more closely aligned with the A/B group. Taking this perspective, it is essential to recognize two things: first, that the middle class population is the majority in Mexico—a fact that has transcendental implications both conceptually and politically speaking—and second, that although Mexico's politicians tend to think of the country as an essentially poor society, the reality is that the majority of the population displays behaviors that suggest otherwise—and this undoubtedly has enormous transcendental effects not just on consumption, but on political preferences, voting patterns, and social and individual behavior.

Therefore, the middle class reflects a segment of the population that values the socioeconomic status they achieved and anticipates further growth. For formal academics, this characterization no doubt remains imprecise; for political and electoral strategists, however, and for more than a few marketing experts, such characterizations can make the difference between won and lost elections, and between viable businesses and those that are unlikely to succeed.

In sum, the middle class in Mexico can be understood as a group comprised of multiple social strata whose common characteristics are essentially cultural, sharing attitudes and consumption patterns.

1.1 The middle class throughout history

In general terms, those who discuss social classes are referring to a form of stratification that classifies a population by income (or expenditure) level, by their position in the production structure, or by those characteristics that differentiate some groups of the population from others. Stratification is something common to all societies in which significant differences exist between distinct strata or groups within the population. The concept of the middle class was born from the need to identify those groups that did not fit neatly within one of the others.

In fact, more than two thousand years ago, Aristotle was already beginning to use the concept of the middle class when he wrote that "in all states there are three elements: one class is very rich, another very poor, and a third in a mean."[2] Karl Marx saw a clash between the exploited and the exploiters, but never acknowledged the existence of other segments of society that did not fit within his rigid vision of social classes. For Marx, the defining factor was ownership of the means of production. However, as Aristotle pointed out, there is a portion of society that doesn't fit within the definitions of either owners or workers (in Marxist terms, exploiter and exploited). Perhaps the error of Marx's prediction stemmed from his dialectical vision of class struggle: the expansion of the uncomfortable middle class made difficult, if not impossible, the sharpening of the contradictions necessary for the development of the dictatorship of the proletariat.

Signaling the limitation of Marx's arguments in the Mexican context becomes ever more important as his arguments are all too often used by radical, and sometimes not-so-radical, political groups to dismiss any attempt at demonstrating progress and focusing on the middle class as opposed to only the poor.

[2] Manuel Briceño Jáuregui, D.J., *La Política, Aristóteles, version directa del original griego*, Panamericana Editorial in 2000, Sanatafé de Bogotá, p. 188.

There have always been individuals who engage in activities that could be classified as middle class

In Marx's time, class divisions were rigid, the differences between them profound and obvious to all. For example, during the industrial revolution, the polarization in both wealth and behavior between the owners of the incipient factories and their workers were extreme and quite visible, giving rise to conflicts directly linked to the conditions experienced by each class.

Nevertheless, one very worthwhile element of Marxism is that of class-consciousness: the role that a person plays in the process of production determines his or her worldview—or, in Marx's terminology, his or her class-consciousness. Members of the middle class are also identified by a vision of their position in the world, both present and future.

Beyond formal definitions, recent world history has shown that societies tend to be differentiated in ways that have little or nothing to do with the social origins of their members. Various sociological studies have shown that, in general terms, individuals bind themselves to those with similar characteristics and patterns of behavior—thus building much of what constitutes a social class.

There have always been individuals who engage in activities that could be classified as middle class. If one were to go back to the Roman or Aztec empires when those societies ceased to be dependent on hunting, became sedentary, and were beginning to organize themselves, one would find that natural distinctions began to appear in social and production-related activities: merchants appeared, as did administrators and teachers. Little by little, a segment of society developed that was not directly involved in the physical production of goods. Such activities represent the beginnings of what we today consider the middle class.

Likewise, insofar as modern societies have become urbanized and a significant part of their economic growth has occurred in the service sector, unanticipated phenomena have surfaced. While the divisions between owners and workers used to be quite obvious, the current differences between workers in any given office are less so. The growth of urban society gave rise to a new social group, characterized principally by the very fact of its members living in an urban setting and sharing both the benefits as well as the costs of city life.

In this way, other professions have appeared—professions that share the quality of not being directly linked to material production: accountants, lawyers, monks, soldiers, etc. Of course, a predetermined economic status isn't necessarily conferred on all of these professions or the people who practice them. However, these activities are typically performed by people who today consider themselves part of the middle class.

Lastly, although many government leaders across the globe have come from business, military, or union backgrounds, the structures of their governments depend on administrators or officials who tend to hold those professions for their entire careers. In big cities, where government functions are concentrated (such as Mexico City, Beijing, Washington, or Paris), the population dedicated to government-related activities tends to expand rapidly. Likewise, in cities that are hubs of financial activity (such as New York and Hong Kong), professions dedicated to financial services proliferate (lawyers, consultants, and various other intermediaries). Once an urban population begins to increase, its political importance also grows and governments dedicate time and resources to the wellbeing of its members.

1.2 Political stability and the middle class

Beyond its characteristic attitudes, the middle class can play a double role in the development of a country: the middle class seeks political stability, but at the same time it is capable of instigating economic changes that enable its members to achieve a better quality of life. One of the great paradoxes of poverty is that those who live in it are often not aware of the risks of abrupt economic or political change–or at least, extremely poor individuals often lack the means to organize themselves to achieve political goals. People and families who have finally achieved some level of minimal economic comfort, on the other hand, tend to value stability and are more likely to reject—for better or for worse—any kind of change that could threaten what they have acquired.

The middle class seeks political stability, but at the same time it is capable of instigating economic changes that enable its members to achieve a better quality of life

THE TRIUMPH OF FELIPE CALDERÓN IN 2006

There are many circumstances that led to Felipe Calderón's triumph in Mexico's 2006 presidential elections, but one rarely discussed—yet very relevant—is the transformation of Mexican society in recent years. For many, Calderón's victory is explained by the mistakes of his chief opponent, López Obrador—mistakes that, no doubt, were a central factor in the outcome of the elections. However, it is impossible to ignore that Mexico is becoming a majority middle-class society, which is something López Obrador obviously failed to realize.

The story of the 2006 presidential election reveals much about how Mexico has changed. According to various polls, those whose families earned less than nine times the minimum wage and those whose families earned more than 15 times the minimum wage decided who they would vote for relatively early in the election process and rarely changed their minds during following months. The group in between—the group whose family incomes were between nine and 15 times the minimum wage, wavered throughout the election cycle, but most ended up voting for Felipe Calderón (or at least not voting for López Obrador) and thus determined the outcome of the election. The paradox is, as always, that the indecisive decide the outcome of close elections.

According to public opinion analysts, the group that changed their minds at various points can be characterized by factors such as the following: they bought homes in the years preceding the election; they had credit cards that were nearly maxed out; they understood that their children's success depended largely on computer skills, high levels of education, and speaking other languages (Labastida was right about this six years prior); they had cars; they traveled; and they sought to systematically elevate their consumption capacities. Apparently the concept of the middle class is elastic, and can encompass those who have barely met the minimum conditions and are at risk of losing what they have achieved, just as it encompasses those who live in relative comfort and do not face similar risks.
López Obrador focused his campaign on the population whose families earned less than

nine times the minimum wage, while Calderón focused his own campaign on the population who felt that any economic change would result in a crisis for their families. In other words, the candidate from the Party of the Democratic Revolution (the PRD) focused on playing to his political base, while the now-president dedicated himself to winning over those voters who were prepared to change their minds. This explains how despite the fact that many who voted for Calderón may have actually preferred López Obrador's rhetoric, their vote was influenced by their condition as members of the middle-class.

In other words, the middle classes are the ones who tend to suffer the most from the consequences of revolutions and other kinds of instability—this is why they constitute a fundamental pillar of democracy and gradual change. The middle classes fear revolutions because they threaten to destroy their families, eat into their incomes and undermine their purchasing power. In Mexico, the middle class has felt the consequences of the financial crises more than any other social group. It's no coincidence that their political inclination is to be conservative and to reject any alternative that could destabilize their security.

Fascism and Nazism were each closely associated with the European middle classes, serving as a means to consolidate authoritarian and abusive regimes that then became militaristic and violent. Without the complicity of the middle class their political experiments—seeking social control, manipulation and mobilization—would not have been possible. The same could be said of other similar movements, even non-violent and non-militaristic ones, which share the same objective: social control and manipulation. This is the story of some populist governments that have taken power in Latin America, some of which are not far removed ideologically from the Italian or Spanish brands of fascism. Historically, urban populations formed the clientelistic foundations for both governments of the right and left. The great masses of poor city dwellers were a natural target for political and partisan activism from all segments of the political spectrum. As in Europe, the capacity for manipulation in Latin

Democracy naturally fits the characteristics of the middle class

America was characterized by caudillos and dictators with great rhetorical abilities. In some Latin American nations, like Argentina with Perón, these movements became permanent features of the political landscape. In others, the movements were limited to certain historical eras.

Mass society began to take hold in the 1930s and 40s in Mexico and other similar countries, becoming a tempting target for manipulation and the formation of a dependent, or paternalistic, political relationship with society. Subsidies, aid, restrictions and other mechanisms quickly turned urban masses into a political instrument. This happened in countries as diverse as Argentina, Brazil, Chile and Mexico, but the phenomena have not always been permanent.

Societies change, income levels rise, new generations bring new values and ideas, sources of information multiply and, little by little, new ways of seeing things emerge. Governments can manipulate populations with little education and few or no alternative sources of information, but the capacity to sustain this strategy tends to diminish with political maturation. Bit by bit, groups connected to such systems of political manipulation shrink in size, and although they may remain large in absolute terms, the population that has relatively higher earnings and defined social aspirations differentiates itself from manipulative governments and leaders. Over time, the urban middle classes that do not require subsidies or depend on them for survival begin to see their future independently from the government.

Today, there is no doubt that democracy is a natural fit with the characteristics of the middle class. The access this group has to information technology brings with it changes in attitudes, a sense of freedom, and therefore a disinclination to support leaders and politicians whose strength resides in an absence of information and knowledge.

In fact, achieving a middle-class life implies fundamental changes of attitude and perception. Access to the Internet affords the opportunity to look in on other worlds and find examples of new ways of life, to learn new ways of doing things, new ways of living, and new ways of becoming involved in politics through social networks. All of this brings a change of attitude, a sense of liberation, and therefore an indisposition to follow leaders and politicians whose strength is based in the absence of information and knowledge.

A person's change from being part of a mass movement to a sense that he is the owner of his own politicization has the potential to transform society. It is a slow process, but a noticeable one that, over time, influences political developments. When that happens, deliberative democracy can grow stronger. At its heart, the strengthening of a middle-class society does not just confer increased stability—it also results in people having the opportunity to develop themselves and, in the process, acquire greater political freedoms.

The change in political preferences observed in Mexico in recent years is also an indication of the growth of the middle class, the reduction of corporativism, and the growth of civic participation: the number of independent voters (those who do not identify themselves with any one particular party) grew from 29% in 1989 to nearly 40% in 2007. [3] This, combined with the high levels of volatility in these voters, shows that Mexicans, feeling that their once-preferred parties no longer represent them, are now inclined to either switch parties, or, increasingly, not align themselves with any party. The recent gubernatorial election results in July of 2010 (especially in Oaxaca, Puebla and Sinaloa, but also in states where the Institutional Revolutionary Party, or PRI, beat the incumbent parties) are indicative of the increase in independent voters across the country. These are states that are traditionally thought of as rural and poor, but are today less so.

Yet, democracy alone does not guarantee the growth and permanence of the middle class. It is essential to increase the rate of economic growth in order to guarantee that an increasing number of Mexicans can achieve a more stable socioeconomic status. For Mexico, the main economic challenge is to increase productivity. In order to achieve this, a society must abandon those activities that generate little value and shift to more profitable activities, a transformation that can only happen when the growing middle class sees stability as a precondition to change rather than a means to preserve the status quo.

The change in political preferences is an indication of the growth of Mexico's middle class

[3] Moreno, Alejandro. *La decisión electoral: Votantes, partidos y democracia en México*, Miguel Ángel Porrúa, 2009, México DF.

Less Mexicans Identify with a Political Party

PARTY IDENTIFICATION[4]

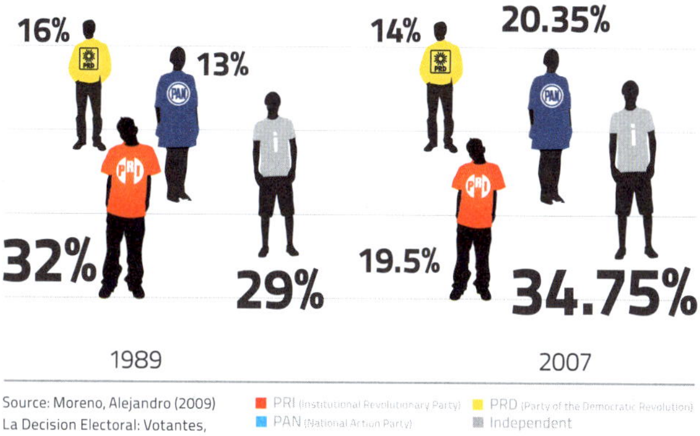

Source: Moreno, Alejandro (2009) La Decision Electoral: Votantes, partidos y democracia en México"
Note: Apolitical and non-voting Mexicans are not included

[4] A center-right party, the National Action Party, or PAN, was founded in 1939 and was traditionally considered the "loyal opposition" to Mexico's long-ruling PRI. Though it was tolerated along with other opposition parties throughout the PRI's 71 years in power, the PAN was never permitted to win a significant election until its first gubernatorial win in 1989. The PAN became the first party to defeat the PRI and break its strangle-hold on the presidency in 2000 with Vicente Fox, a relative party outsider with a successful career as CEO of Coca-Cola, as their candidate. The PAN won again in a tight election in 2006 with the current President Felipe Calderón. Presently, the PAN holds eight state governorships and 143 out of 500 members of Congress and 50 of the 128 Senate seats.

Formed after the devastating Mexican Revolution (1910-1920) and the period of political instability that followed, the Institutional Revolutionary Party, or PRI, was created in an effort to prevent further violence among rival political groups. Organizing and incorporating broad sectors of society, the PRI stayed in power through a combination of party discipline and government largess supplemented with electoral manipulation and ideological swings intended to reflect society. The PRI dominated for decades, holding all state governorships until 1989, a majority in both congressional chambers until 1997, and the presidency until 2000. After losing the presidency again in 2006, the party swept the 2009 congressional elections and now represents the largest faction in the Chamber of Deputies with 240 seats and the second largest in the Senate with 33 seats. They also now have 19 state governorships.

In the 1980s, a group of left-leaning pro-reform priístas who believed the party had become calcified and hierarchical split with the PRI and, together with a coalition of the traditional leftist parties (Communists, Trotskyites, etc.) formed what would become the Party of the Democratic Revolution, or PRD. Cuauhtémoc Cárdenas, the son of one of the founders of the PRI, lost his bid for the presidency in 1988 to the PRI (who many believe stole the election). The allegations of fraud consolidated the party, which is strongest in Central and Southern Mexico, where it holds five governorships, the mayorship of Mexico City, and the majority of the Mexico City Assembly. At present, there are 25 PRD senators and 72 deputies. In 2006, PRD candidate Andrés Manuel López Obrador lost the presidential election by just .58 percent. López Obrador and his supporters denounced the election as fraudulent, though the Federal Electoral Institute (IFE) rejected this claim based on a partial recount and other evidence. López Obrador refused to accept the results, a tactic that led to party infighting that the PRD continues to work to overcome. Many of the ongoing divisions within the party go back to the two contingents that originally founded the party: the former left of the PRI (which remains state-centric) and the traditional left (which has evolved towards modern social democratic politics).

In order to promote the existence of a middle class that advocates for change within the context of a stable democratic society, it is essential to have an educational system and other mechanisms to provide ongoing professional training that prepare people to successfully confront the natural fear of change. Thus, a certain degree of schizophrenia is required of the middle class: it must be in favor of political, macroeconomic and juridical stability—but only insofar as they enable change, a "revolution" in productivity, creativity, the creation of wealth, and the discovery of fundamental comparative advantages.

In fact, development is the result of a volatile process that attains its ultimate expression in the form of democracy. Of course, many in Asia think democracy is not a requisite for development—some even see it as an obstacle. If Mexico achieves future success, it will be an example of modernization through the growth of the middle class and civic participation. Unfortunately, it remains unclear and uncertain whether those political and economic interest groups that benefit from maintaining the status quo will allow the average Mexican to freely employ his or her talents and thus achieve authentic development.

1.3 Two middle classes: entitlement versus merit

In Mexico, members of middle class households can earn incomes that fall anywhere between a few to many dozens of times the minimum wage. In other words, they can be almost in the top decile on the national income scale, or several deciles below it. Two families living in the same residential area and earning similar incomes can have dramatically different spending capacities based on the number of dependents living within their households. For these reasons, many academics prefer to use the plural form, "middle classes," in recognition of the diversity found within the group.

However it is denominated, the fact is that the Mexican middle class is made up of multiple earning levels and a diversity of backgrounds, professions, and social groups. Just as there are families who have been part of the urban middle class for many generations, there are families who have only recently emigrated from rural areas. These factors have a strong impact on the ways in which members of the middle class behave, vote, and view the world around them. Subgroups within the same segment of the population, over time, have tended to assimilate and form what is commonly known as "the middle class."

Historically, two of the fundamental sources of the development of the Mexican middle class were the government bureaucracy and trade unions. Bureaucrats earned stable incomes that, bit by bit, allowed them to lead comfortable—and even privileged—lives. The same was true for workers who belonged to powerful large private or public company unions whose sources of work were essentially immune to the country's economic changes.

The members of the middle class who came from such backgrounds developed a strong dependency on the government and are the pillar of support for continued entitlements, including direct subsidies and protection from competition. One needs only to consider the selling of positions within entities like Pemex (the state oil company), Luz y Fuerza del Centro (the electricity provider which no longer exists), the Federal Electricity Commission or the Secretariat of Public Education to identify a worldview typical of this social group—a worldview that also consists of protecting privileges that, in many cases, are passed from one generation to another, a trait typical in corporativism and clientelism.

For strategic reasons, the middle class associated with corporativism frequently endorses a proletarian rhetoric, not so much in defense or support of the rights of the poor, but rather to preserve their privileged condition.

The other fundamental source of Mexico's middle class is quite the opposite: people who have worked hard as productive laborers, emigrants, or members of the informal economy who haven't appropriated anything they haven't earned, and budding businesspeople who have dedicated themselves to systematically—if precariously—improving their situations, not by exploiting privileges but by assuming daily risks. This is a segment of society whose members stake it all every day—people who seek business opportunities, people who would move to Cancun if they think better business opportunities can be found there just as easily as they might instead move to Chicago in search of a better life. These people tend to develop a strong work ethic, search for new opportunities for their families, view competition as a natural part of life, and staunchly criticize the government and taxes.

THE CREATIVE CLASS

In 2002, the urban studies theorist Richard Florida wrote a book titled *The Rise of the Creative Class*. His central thesis states that in developed countries a group emerges whose professional activities are based on knowledge and creativity. Although members of the creative class can belong to any industry, in the heart of this group are scientists, engineers, university professors, poets, novelists, artists, designers, architects, programmers and researchers.

Many have criticized the concept of a "creative class" because they believe that creativity is universal and because this cluster of "creative" people does not see itself as a group. That is, they have no class consciousness. Nonetheless, members of the creative class do share an identity based on consumption patterns, work habits and preferences about where and how to live.

For example, most of the members of the creative class are not owners of any significant property in a physical sense. Their property is an intangible good that is literally in their heads. The creative class values openness and diversity, and this has implications in the workplace, in public policy, and in the daily exchange between companies and this group of consumers.

The creative class values things that go far beyond income and job security; they value challenge and responsibility, but also flexibility and their involvement in society.

The creative class cannot conceive itself outside the concept of a city. The "creatives" gain force as a group as they interact more and more with each other: the available knowledge base and the possibilities for innovation are exponential when people exchange ideas.

The creative class seeks to live in places within walking distance of shops, restaurants and parks, and where interaction and the exchange of ideas are easy. In Mexico City, the creative class lives in neighborhoods like Coyoacan, La Condesa and La Roma ... versus chic but soulless neighborhoods like Mexico City's Santa Fe.

From a business perspective, catering to the creative class means understanding that this is a very diverse group. So, for example, an establishment that aims to cater to this sector must take into account that people with different sexual preferences, national origins, and so-called bohemians should all feel at home.

Since success in the XXI century will be governed by knowledge and creativity, it is important to create the conditions required to encourage the middle class to generate greater value.

Written by Verónica Baz

Reduced fertility rates and economic stability have been key in the development of the middle class

For some in this group, remittances have become not just a source of economic improvement, but of social mobility. Households receiving wages earned by a family member outside of Mexico tend to save more and to improve their spending and investment levels. In some way, the very fact of knowing there is a possibility of emigrating, of leaving behind their social and geographical ties, turns them into aspiring or real members of the middle class. Amartya Sen argues in *Development as Freedom*[5] that development occurs when one has the freedom to choose—even within certain boundaries—which path to follow.

Stability, both economic and financial (above all the absence of episodes of widespread financial ruin), and the recent significant decline in fertility rates have been key to the development of the middle class in Mexico.

Moreover, trade openness and the North American Free Trade Agreement (NAFTA) dramatically reduced the costs of goods for Mexican families at the same time that the quality and variety of goods and services in the country grew. The Wal-Mart phenomenon, for example, has transformed consumption, lowering the prices of food, clothing, and shoes. Hand-in-hand with this came the liberalization of the mortgage market and the explosion of consumer credit (automobiles, credit cards, department stores). Budget airlines opened air transport to millions of people who before traveled only by bus; the same is true for universities like the UVM-UNITEC and TEC Milenio— institutions designed to serve this population.[6] The success of these products and services, which are aimed directly at the middle class, is evidence that economic stability is far more transcendent than many imagine.

5 Sen, Amartya, *Development as Freedom*, Random House, 1999, New York.

6 UVM-UNITEC and TEC Milenio are three of the many recently created universities that directly target lower-middle-class students. UVM-UNITEC is owned by the US-based Laureate Group.

The most important factor, however, which makes development depend on individuals and families rather than the government, is the decrease in fertility rates and resulting smaller-sized families. Today's fertility rate is just 2.05 children per fertile mother–in comparison to the 1960s, when the rate reached 7.3. The lower rate is both the cause and the consequence of the expansion of the middle class. The principal drivers of the reduced fertility rate are emigration from rural areas to cities, and the growing participation of women in the workforce. In addition, when a family has fewer children, the average productivity of each child must rise–creating incentives for families to invest time and resources in their children's education, health, and professional development.

1.4 The Mexican middle class in a global context

It is perfectly logical to ask what two families, or two individuals, with salary differentials up to ten times one another, could possibly have in common; the answer is that they share many of the attributes typically used to define the middle class.

In the international environment, many middle class people and families have income and savings levels that allow them ample freedom to consume. The Mexican middle class, though, has not yet necessarily attained the living standards enjoyed by the international middle class. But, despite the differences in their incomes, these two middle classes share a common view of life and of their place in society.

According to *The Economist* (2009),[7] in many of the so-called emerging nations, the middle classes have grown over the past 15 years, representing nearly half the populations in countries like China, Brazil, Chile, Mexico–and, within another 10 or 15 years, India will likely achieve the same. The Economist proposes an unconventional definition of the middle class. It examines the population's behavior and makes international comparisons. The results of this exercise suggest there are actually two populations that can be called middle-class: one is a domestic middle class, and the other is transnational. The distinction is important because it leads to an understanding that the concepts normally associated with the middle class serve to identify a broader population than is traditionally perceived.
The publication's analysis makes reference to the U.S. psychologist, Abra-

[7] "Two billion more bourgeois," *The Economist* (print edition), February 12, 2009.

ham Maslow, who many decades ago created a hierarchy of human behaviors based on needs. According to Maslow, a human being starts by resolving his fundamental problems, such as housing and food; once he has achieved both, he concerns himself with things that are increasingly less basic. After addressing the essentials, those who are part of the middle class still have about one-third of their incomes left over for discretionary spending. Finally, *The Economist's* report points out that this segment of the population has a daily income of between ten and one hundred dollars. Evidently, the disparity in the numbers gets at the heart of the problem: reaching a middle-class consumption level is very different in New York than in Chennai, Guangzhou, Brasilia or Morelia.

The criteria established by *The Economist* leads one to consider as "middle-class" anyone who consumes and possesses goods that are associated with middle-class behavior. Among them are a home, an automobile, consumer appliances (refrigerator, washing machine, computer, telephone), access to health care and recreational travel—in other words, all the trappings of a modern urban lifestyle.

Mexico's middle class distinguishes itself from its international peers in one fundamental way: in contrast to the transnational middle class, Mexico's middle class families have attained this status by combining the incomes of various family members rather than through the increased income of an individual or couple.

The advancement has been real, which is why it is important to fortify the sources of economic stability that have enabled the growth of the middle class. It is necessary to transform the structure of the Mexican economy in

Mexican families have attained their middle class status thanks to the combination of several family members' incomes

order to achieve elevated economic growth rates that, in turn, will strengthen and accelerate the development of Mexico as a middle-class society. The causality is bidirectional: growth is indispensable to the expansion of the middle class, but sustained growth requires a broad middle class.

This bidirectionality explains the potential for multiple points of equilibrium. On one hand is a situation in which progress becomes impossible, Mexico falls into the development trap and its population is stuck responding to the lack of growth by saying "*ni modo*," or "oh well." This option would leave Mexico with a limited middle class. On the other hand is a situation in which robust development is achieved and growth and the middle class create a feedback loop, each accelerating the other.

The remaining differences between the Mexican middle class and the transnational middle class represent specific challenges for Mexico on its path to expanding its middle class base. Besides ensuring political stability, the data shows that the larger a country's middle class population is, the greater its potential for economic growth and, therefore, development.

* * *

What is the middle class?

- The concept of a middle class is very elastic because it includes people with very different incomes.
- There have always been individuals with professions that may be classified as 'middle class'.
- The middle class seeks political stability and it is capable of promoting economic changes to improve quality of life.
- Democracy fits naturally with the characteristics of the middle class.
- A change in a society's political preferences is a symptom of the growth of the middle class.
- Economic stability and a reduction in fertility rates have been key in the development of the middle class.
- Families have reached middle class status thanks to the combined incomes of multiple family members.

To a middle-class society: measures of the transformation

Chapter 2

Mexicans often take a fearful view of the future, imagining catastrophes and difficult times ahead. Years of recurring crises and bad governments–or, at least, incapable or inadequate governments–have left Mexicans with a pessimistic vision of the future and with an attitude of *"ni modo,"* or "oh well." What is interesting is that objective reality contradicts, in part, such perceptions. In today's Mexico, the possibility of stimulating greater individual and family progress exists, whether through the accumulation of human capital, participation in business activities–including informal ones–or emigration.

If instead of looking forward with apprehension, Mexican society observed and accepted its own progress, the implications would be quite the opposite: despite errors, problems, concerns and complaints, the reality is that there have been very significant changes in the lives of many Mexicans that are seldom recognized. In reality, the country has experienced profound changes in practically all of its structures and characteristics.

In addition to the traditional measurements of poverty and income distribution, there is extensive data confirming the significant progress achieved in Mexico and the expansion of its middle class (with recognition that the progress is still precarious and insufficient). Some illustrative indicators are included here.

This chapter explores the changes at an aggregate level: how the economy has grown, mortality rates changed, life expectancy increased, and how, in general, the quality of life has improved for many millions of Mexicans.

2.1 Characteristics of a more robust middle class

First, the economic progress experienced by Mexico's middle class will be analyzed. Although far more elevated growth rates in recent decades would have been preferable, the fact remains that the Mexican economy has indeed achieved rates of growth that have changed the country.

Though per capita incomes has grown slowly in Mexico over the past three decades, resulting in the consolidation of the middle class, it is important to situate Mexico in an international context, particularly vis-à-vis its competitors.

The following graph shows how Mexico still has some ways to go in achieving the advances in per capita income other countries have attained in the past three decades.

Evolution of Mexico's GDP per capita

(2003 PESOS)

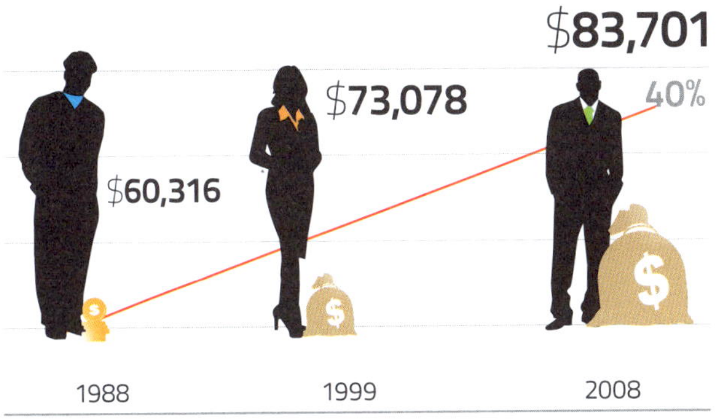

Sources: INEGI (National Institute of Statistics and Geography) and CONAPO (National Population Council).

Although there is room for improvement, the positive implications of Mexico's change over time in per capita GDP translate to improved life expectancy and quality of life for Mexicans.

An alternative explanation—one that has not been sufficiently investigated—is that the growth of the middle class is indicative of a systematic underestimating of GDP and growth rates. Although INEGI has already corrected this as of 2007, perhaps it has not done so sufficiently.

Mexico's Economic Growth Lags Behind Other Countries

GROWTH IN GROSS DOMESTIC PRODUCT, 1980-2010

BASE 1980=1

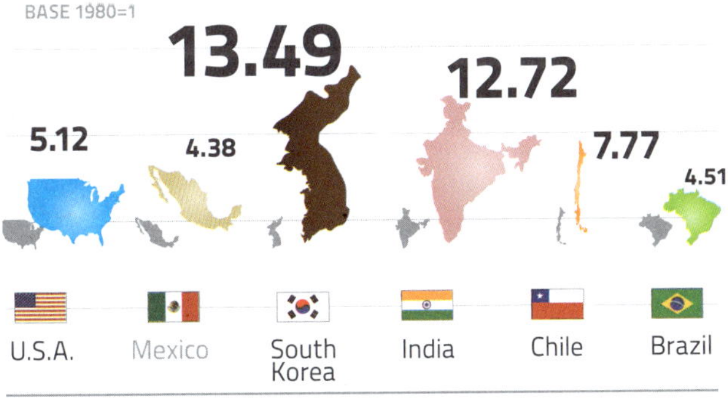

Source: IMF, World Economic Outlook.

GDP measurements were revised in order to increase accuracy. With these revisions, total nominal GDP increased, on average, 12 percent. This means the previous methodology did not include a significant portion of the value-added of the Mexican economy. There is insufficient data to carry out the same comparison for other years, since only in the 2003-2007 period do the old and new methodologies overlap. It is possible that the difference between the GDP measured on the basis of the 1993 and the 2003 methodologies could be close to 15 percent in 2010. This correction - perhaps still partial by not considering the informal economy or the transformation of the economy since 2003 - is consistent with the hypothesis of the book, that of a growing middle class. The upward revision of Mexico's GDP is a highly relevant economic development; yet it has been poorly disseminated.

In this context, it is important to understand the evolution of poverty levels, since much of the Mexican population falls in this category. It's true that poverty has been steadily and systematically decreasing, except as a result of economic and financial crises, including the most recent one in 2009. After steady success in lowering poverty levels, the spike observed in 2008 should be viewed as a warning signal. Expanding the middle class to encompass the broad majority of the population remains an elusive goal.

Nominal Gross Domestic Product

BILLIONS OF PESOS

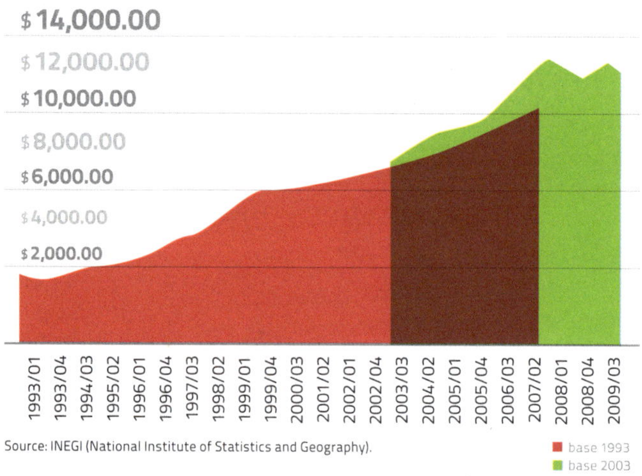

Source: INEGI (National Institute of Statistics and Geography).

The increase in GDP per capita translates into longer life expectancy and improved quality of life for Mexicans

On the other hand, it is also necessary to acknowledge that just a half-century ago, 80% of Mexicans were poor, and thus, so was the entire country. Today, the majority is not poor and by extension, neither is the country—although there is still widespread poverty. The progress that has been achieved, although at insufficient levels, shows that Mexico should aspire to eradicate widespread poverty within a generation, having at least 80% of the population not in poverty.

What can this positive tendency in poverty reduction and the growth of the middle class be attributed to? Mexican society has changed in many ways in recent years, and each change has brought improvements in its own category.

Although widespread poverty still exists, Mexico is no longer a poor country

Poverty Has Declined

PERCENTAGE OF POPULATION IN POVERTY

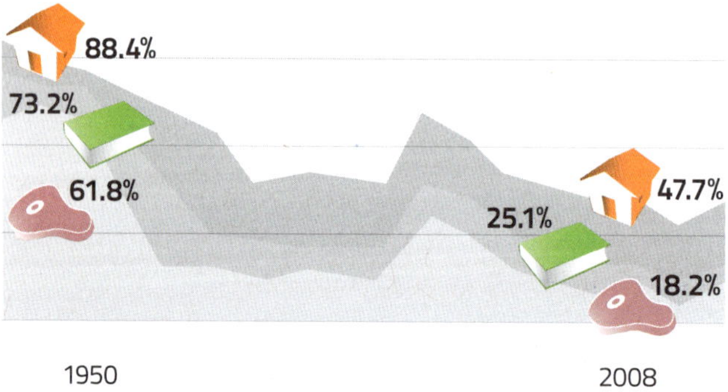

Fuente: Source: CONEVAL(National Council for the Evaluation of Social Development Policy)

Note: Food Poverty means lacking access to sufficient nutrition, Capacity Poverty signifies sufficient income for food, but lacking income for education and health, and Patrimonial Poverty includes sufficient income for food, education and health, but not enough income to purchase needed clothing and household goods.

- Patrimonial Poverty
- Capacity Poverty
- Food Poverty

Among other things, macroeconomic stability, the absence of wealth destruction, the absence of a decrease in real wages since 1996, along with spending growth on social programs like Oportunidades[8] have contributed positively to the improvement in quality of life for Mexicans.

POVERTY AND TRANSFERS

As shown in the following table, an analysis of 2008 earned income data from the National Household Income and Expenditure Survey (known as the ENIGH in Spanish), monetary income accounted for 80.1% of total quarterly income of households, while non-cash income contributed the remaining 19.9%. The loss in total household income between 2006 and 2008 (-1.6%) was derived mainly from the reduction in income from property rental (-46%), and a decrease in in-kind transfers (-22%).

[8] Oportunidades, or Opportunities, is a poverty alleviation program, begun in 2002, that offers conditional cash payments to low income families, based on the fulfillment of requirements such as school attendance and health center visits for their children.

Total Nominal Income
By Principal Source of income

(QUARTERLY AVERAGE* AND QUARTERLY VARIANCE BY HOUSEHOLD, PRICES IN 2008 PESOS)

SOURCES	NACIONAL INCOME 2002	2004	2006	2008	VARIATION % 2006 - 2008
Total Nominal Income	**32,773**	**33,872**	**37,299**	**36,694**	**-1.6**
Nominal Monetary Income	**25,889**	**26,889**	**29,221**	**29,401**	**0.6**
Employee Wages	16,387	17,302	18,216	18,318	0.6
Income from independent work	2,664	2,674	3,181	4,680	47.1
Other work income	467	593	861	939	9.2
Property rental	3,589	3,126	3,307	1,771	-46.4
Transfers	2,742	3,178	3,636	3,669	0.9
Other nominal income	40	16	20	24	20.3
Non-monetary Nominal Income	**6,884**	**6,983**	**8,078**	**7,292**	**-9.7**
Self-consumption	302	252	299	305	1.9
In-kind Wages	597	539	580	545	-6.1
In-Kind Transfers	2,000	2,082	3,005	2,352	-21.7
Estimated Value of Housing Rental	3,984	4,109	4,194	4,091	-2.5

*In calculating average income one takes in consideration the total number of households at the national level.
Source: Mexico's National Institute of Statistics, INEGI, "Communicado No. 191/09" July 16, 2009 Aguascalientes, Mexico.

Non-monetary income is particularly important in the calculation of income distribution and poverty in Mexico, given that this component represents a larger share of total income earned in the first-decile households, that is, in households with low income.

A detailed analysis of in-kind transfer data (in real terms) demonstrates that, on average, in 2006, households received $ 3,005 pesos in these transfers per quarter, an amount that dropped to $ 2,352 pesos in 2008. The decline may be a case of seasonality, due to high levels of spending by political parties during the 2006 election. Therefore, the income of households in the election year is not comparable to the year before or after, when families did not receive income from election spending.

The presidential election accentuated in-kind transfers, particularly among the low-income population

The 2006 presidential election also seems to have influenced the number of Mexican households that received in-kind transfers, so that, between 2004 and 2006, the number of families who benefited from these revenues increased by 2.6 million, while between 2006 and 2008, approximately 1.8 million households stopped receiving these benefits.

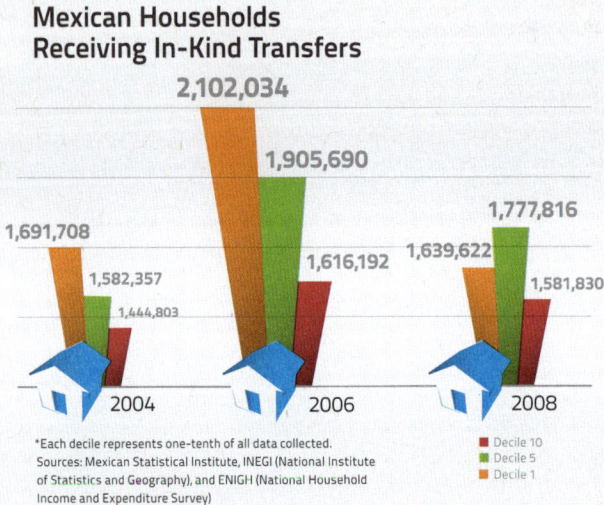

Mexican Households Receiving In-Kind Transfers

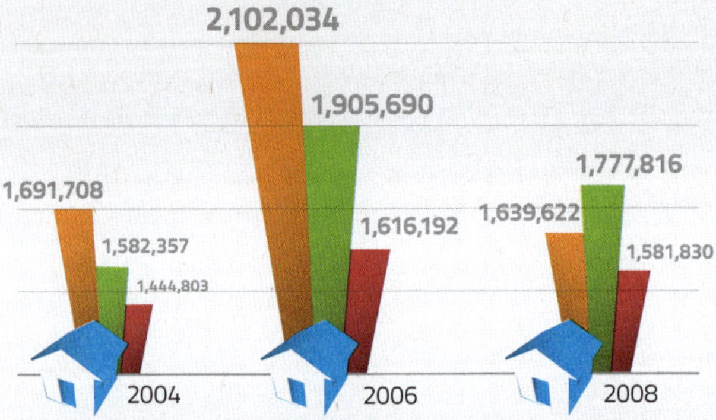

*Each decile represents one-tenth of all data collected.
Sources: Mexican Statistical Institute, INEGI (National Institute of Statistics and Geography), and ENIGH (National Household Income and Expenditure Survey)

Transfers Increase in Presidential Election Years

VARIATION IN THE NUMBER OF HOUSES THAT RECEIVE TRANSFERS

DECILE	2006 vs 2004	2008 vs 2006
TOTAL	2,634,282	-1,799,130
I	410,326	-462,412
II	371,128	-378,137
III	244,952	-145,334
IV	338,735	-200,433
V	323,333	-127,874
VI	213,662	-148,580
VII	248,942	-168,780
VIII	162,309	-57,015
IX	149,506	-76,203
X	171,389	-34,362

*Note: In-kind transfers (gifts): homes
Sources: Mexican Statistical Institute, INEGI (National Institute of Statistics and Geography), and ENIGH (National Household Income and Expenditure Survey)

Perhaps the main result of these in-kind transfers is related to the redistributive effect of these resources on the income of Mexican households. As can be seen in the graphs below, the elections caused a spike in in-kind transfers, particularly for the portions of the population with low incomes.

Given these results, it can be argued that both the pronounced decline in poverty between 2004 and 2006, as well as the increase registered between 2006 and 2008 are both overestimated as a result of the large in-kind transfers of 2006.

To isolate the effect of in-kind transfers or gifts on the incomes of Mexican households, the average income by family or by decile is derived from recurring sources. This calculation of income shows that between 2006 and 2008, the real average income of Mexican families experienced moderate growth, at 0.4%, which contrasts with the 1.6% reduction in real income reported officially.

By decile, real household income without in-kind transfers also contrasts with the official trends. In fact, in the case of each of the lower deciles, with the exception of the third, growth can be observed. This implies that the poverty level in Mexico, including in-kind transfers, neither fell in 2006 as far as was reported, nor increased in 2008 as much as many claimed.

HOUSEHOLD SAVINGS CAPACITY: INFERRING THE SIZE MIDDLE OF MEXICO'S MIDDLE CLASS

An important conclusion derived from ENIGH data relates to the size of the middle class in Mexico, based on a calculation of the average monetary savings capacity of households by decile.

In fact, the survey shows that a significant proportion (60%) of households—average families in the six deciles with the most income—had the capacity to save in 2008, given that their monetary income exceeded their monetary expenditure in the quarter in which the survey was conducted.[9]

In terms of population, this represents a little more than 64 million Mexicans. In contrast, the remaining 40% of the population, on average, needs outside support, or transfers, to cover their monetary expenditure needs.

[9] In 2008, the ENIGH survey was performed between August 21 and November 17. The survey has occurred using the same methodology and definitions since 1992, making the results comparable over that entire period.

The data also reveal that households with the capacity to save significantly increased their financial savings in 2008, compared to 2006. This development may reflect the consumer's perspective on the economic outlook for Mexico and the world, with Mexican households increasing their savings in anticipation of reduced or uncertain future monetary inflows.

This box was developed in collaboration with Manuel Aragonés and Guillermo García

CONEVAL POVERTY NUMBERS AND THE COST OF THE 2008-09 CRISIS

If there was any doubt about the severity of the 2008-09 crisis, the poverty measures in the 2010 National Survey of Household Income Expenditure (ENIGH) conducted by Mexico's official Statistics Institute (INEGI) and its agency to evaluate social development policy (Coneval) confirm the unforgiving nature of the contraction. They do it not so much based on general macroeconomic variables, but in terms of the income, consumption, and budget of Mexican families.

Due to the negative results found by the survey (total income dropped 6.8 percent, income per household decreased 12.3 percent, and per capita income dropped 9.3 percent), most analysts expected an important increase in the number of people living in relative and absolute poverty since 2008. Although the percentage of Mexicans living in poverty did increase, growth was less than expected (based on the methodology used by Coneval since 2008). The proportion of Mexicans living in poverty went up 1.7 percent to 46.2 percent, increasing the number of people living in this condition by 3.2 million.

To determine poverty levels, Coneval considers income per decile as well as six other "deficiencies" as measures of welfare: educational achievement, access to health services, access to social security, housing quality and space, basic housing services, and access to food.

Growth in poverty was less than proportional to the decrease in income because total spending not only did not drop, but actually grew 2.2 percent in real terms. As the number of households increased by 6.28 percent, total current spending per houshold decreased 3.8 percent (much less than the 12 percent decline recorded in total income), and total per capita current income barely dropped, falling only 0.4 percent.

The stability of total current per capita income coupled with the increase in transfers from government programs allowed Mexicans, in particular those in the lower deciles, to have access to the basic necessities used as a baseline for measuring poverty levels. That is to say, even with a lower household or per capita income, there was not an increase, but a decrease in the "deficiencies" Coneval uses to complement income in its multidimensional measurement of poverty.

For each of the "deficiencies" taken into consideration by Coneval there was an improvement between 2008 and 2010, with the exception of access to food. Some 20.6 percent of the population had less than adequate education in 2010, while in 2008 21.9 percent did. The lack of access to health services dropped from 40.8 to 31.8 percent; lack of access to social security from 65.0 to 60.7; lack of housing quality and space, from 17.7 to 15.2; and of basic housing services from 19.2 to 16.5. However, insufficient access to food increased from 21.7 to 24.9 percent.

The decrease in most of the deficiencies is explained by the fact that current total income fell less among the lowest deciles—mostly because spending in these deciles not only did not drop but actually increased.

The most severe fall in current household income happened in the highest deciles (for deciles IX and X, by 11.5 and 17.8 percent respectively; for deciles I and II, by 7.6 and 6.8 percent). In per capita terms, the decrease of current income for deciles I and II was 3.9 and 0.7 percent, while that of deciles IX and X was 8.6 and 13.9 percent.

At the same time, current spending (which is more closely related to welfare levels) fell by a much lesser extent, and in some deciles it even increased. For example, for decile I (the poorest) current spending per household grew 1.2 percent while spending per capita increased 5.5 percent; for decile II, current spending per household dropped 4.6 percent while spending per capita grew 1.7 percent.

The fact that the Mexican Congress and Executive branch have devoted a larger budget for social spending also played a big role in allowing households to reassign their spending in order to soften the fall in income in terms of consumption per capita. In particular, spending on healthcare per household decreased 13.6 percent in ENIGH 2010, which let families spend more in other areas, mostly thanks to the increase in public healthcare coverage.

For all these reasons, Coneval came to the remarkable conclusion that extreme poverty in Mexico not only did not increase, but decreased, going from 10.6 percent in 2008 to 10.4 in 2010. This level is, no doubt, unacceptably high for a country with an annual average per capita income of 10,000 dollars. There can be no excuse for Mexico not being able to decrease extreme poverty by half within a few years.

One of the most interesting aspects of ENIGH 2010, albeit little discussed, is the 6.28 percent growth in the number of households (6.4 in terms of housing units), while the average number of members per household reduced by 3.4 percent, from 4.01 to 3.87 people. The increase in the number of houses and the reduction of the average number of household's members reflect the secular expansion of the middle class, despite the severe crisis, and imply an important welfare improvement in terms of living space.

Analysts that prefer emphasizing a growth in poverty as a result of the crisis use the previous Coneval methodology, based in terms of income, which also allows for longer-term comparisons. With this methodology, patromonial poverty (the broadest concept of poverty) increased between 2008 and 2010, from 47.7 to 51.3 percent, or 3.6 percentage points.

This index is used to argue that Mexico is no longer a middle class country, that most of the people are, again, poor. In this regard, several comments are worth making:

1. ENIGH 2010 measures people's income in the third quarter of that year. If one accepts the premise that as income drops, poverty increases, then it is also true that when income rises, poverty declines. Thus, by the third quarter of 2011, with an average GDP growth of five percent, most Mexicans must be considered middle class again, even with this definition.

2. GDP in 2009 dropped 6.1 percent and patrimonial poverty (measured by income) grew 3.6 percent. As a point of comparison, in 1995, GDP dropped 6.5 percent, but patrimonial poverty grew 16.6 percent between 1994 and 1996.

3. Measuring income through surveys is imperfect, and the underestimation bias can increase in a context of economic turmoil. It is interesting to note that the disassociation of income and spending (this last one did not drop according to ENIGH) is not consistent with Mexico's macroeconomic performance, where income and spending moved pari passu.

   There is extensive literature that confirms the underreporting of income in household surveys. The Economic Commission for Latin America and the Caribbean (ECLAC) recommends an adjustment to make the results of the survey consistent with national accounts.[10] In Mexico's case, it is estimated that the survey's total current income in households represented only 49 percent and 48 percent of their total available income calculated through national accounts in 2008 and 2010. This means, an underreporting of 51 and 52 percent respectively. These adjusted income figures, following ECLAC's recommendation, imply a much lower level of poverty than the one officially reported.

The depth of the crisis, which has been the most severe in the last seventy years at an international level, is not surprising. In Mexico, it was much more than a minor cold. Be it deliberately or not, the countercyclical measures that the Mexican Executive branch pushed in 2009 were not enough to stop the fall of aggregate demand and GDP. However, the deterioration of welfare conditions turned out lower than expected.

In the medium term, Mexico's decision to pursue a conservative macroeconomic policy will be recognized as a success. Mexico is one of the few countries that does not require, after the 2008-09 financial-economic turbulence, a macroeconomic adjustment in terms of debt, public deficit, current account deficit, excessive overvaluation of currency, or international trade openness. Some of the adjustments currently necessary in other parts of the world will imply a greater growth in poverty than the one painfully experienced by many Mexicans between 2008 and 2010.

What is incredible is that, while being conscious of the seriousness of the crisis, its length, and long term effects in developed economies, the Mexican political system has not been able to take advantage of the situation to move forward on any of the crucial reforms that are very much needed to bring about growth.

Even worse, there are those who congratulate themselves on these growing poverty numbers, instead of assuming responsibility for the reforms currently bogged down. Furthermore, given that the approval and implementation of structural reforms would likely bolster investor and consumer confidence and boost economic growth, the political paralysis has also accounted, to some extent, for hindering the optimism of economic agents that is needed to sustain a successful recovery, continue the expansion of the middle class, and overcome extreme poverty in the country.

Written by Luis de la Calle

[10] See "Compendio de mejores prácticas en la medición de pobreza", Grupo de Expertos en Estadísticas de Pobreza, Grupo de Río, 2007, ECLAC. http://www.eclac.org/ilpes/noticias/paginas/2/40352/rio_group_compendium_es.pdf

Besides macroeconomic stability, achievements in public health have contributed to an improved quality of life for Mexicans, as in the case of longer life expectancies, lower fertility rates and a dramatic decrease in the dependency ratio.

Increased Life Expectancy in Mexico

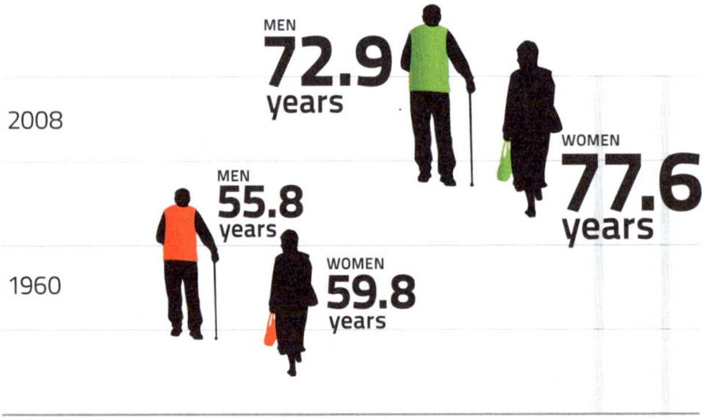

Source: OECD

The increase in life expectancy at birth is, without doubt, the clearest health achievement in recent decades: the average Mexican's life expectancy has risen by approximately four years in just one decade. Women born in 1990 have a life expectancy of 74 years, while it rises to nearly 78 for those born in 2009; for men born in 1990 the life expectancy is 68 years, rising to 73 for those born in 2009.

The same phenomenon can be observed in infants. The probability of a Mexican child dying in its first years of life has dropped considerably. This points to improvements in hospitals, better care for pregnant women and newborns, and improved nutrition.

Infant Mortality in Mexico Has Declined

DEATHS PER ONE THOUSAND BIRTHS

Source: OECD

The following graph shows the impressive decline in mortality from parasitic diseases, which are common in societies with relatively poor hygiene conditions and meager health services.

Death by Parasitic Illnesses

MEXICO

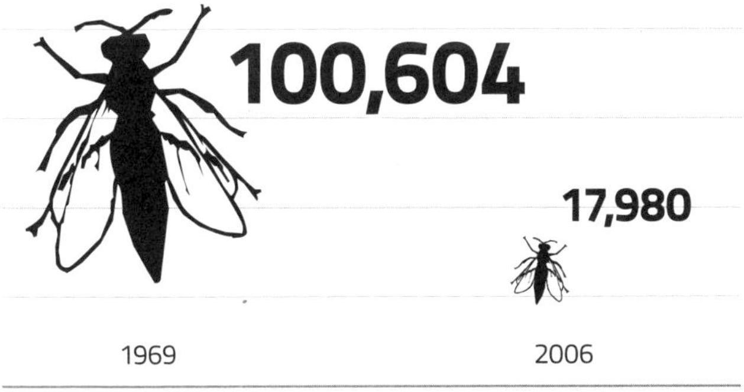

Source: OECD, Health Data, November 2009.

The fact that Mexico has more working-aged people than dependents promotes the accumulation of wealth

Mexicans aren't just living longer lives—they are also dedicating more years of their lives to education. They are able to do this because of the decreased dependency ratio, which in turn boosts Mexicans' capacity to invest greater resources and time into each child within the family.

If one defines dependency ratio as the outcome of dividing the number of minors (up to 20 years of age) and the elderly (above 65 years of age) by the rest of the population[11], the resulting data is as follows:

Inverse of the Dependency Ratio for the Mexican Population

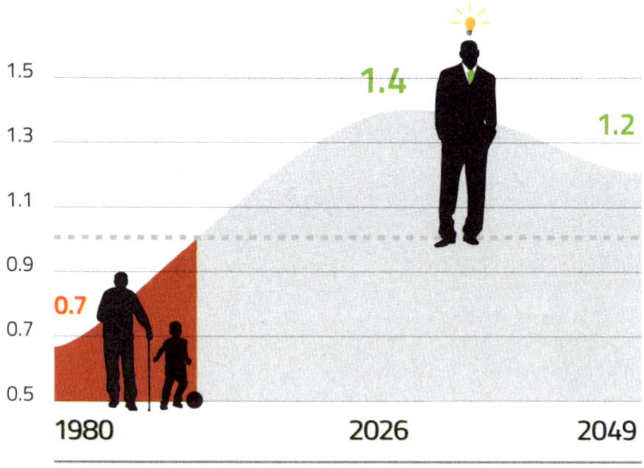

Source: US Census Bureau

[11] Generally, the dependency ratio is calculated using the populations below 15 years of age and above 64. However, for the purposes of this book, it is more effective to count dependents as those up to 20 years of age to emphasize the importance of education in the formation of the middle class and the growth in average productivity.

In the previous graph two phenomena can be appreciated: first, the enormous difficulty for Mexico to invest in its own development during the 1970s and 1980s when a high dependency ratio demanded the spending of the national income on its youth; second, the historic opportunity of having a favorable dependency ratio for a enough years sufficient to reasonably aspire to true development.

Having a favorable dependency ratio means that right now, there are more people of working age than there are dependents (children and elderly). The phenomenon is comparable to having no household debt, few costs (because there are few or no children in the home) and high income (because there are two working adults). The result favors the accumulation of wealth.

In recent decades, the average number of years Mexicans spend in school has doubled (to 8.3 years) at the same time that university enrollment has tripled.

The average number of years of schooling in Mexico doubled

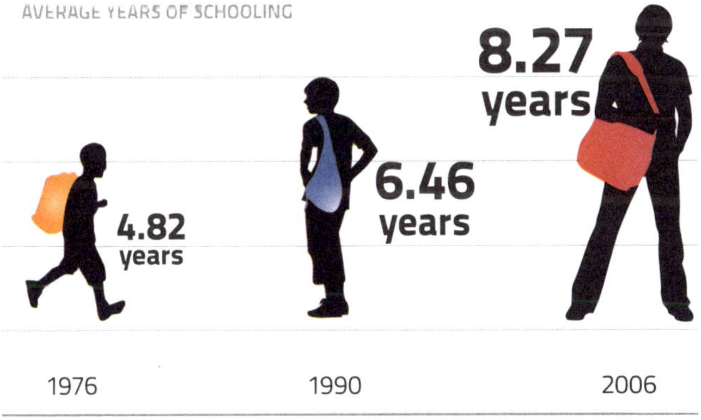

Source: OECD.

It is important to note the sharp increase in university enrollment between 1980 and 2009, along with the positive implications this has for the consolidation of the middle class in the medium and long-terms.

The Number of Students Receiving a Higher Education Tripled

THOUSANDS OF STUDENTS

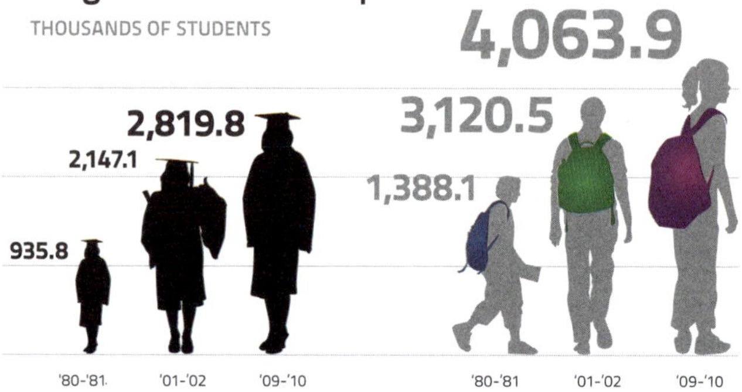

Source: OECD.

■ University
■ High School

Today Mexicans receive more years of schooling and a higher quality education than their parents received

Average Years of Schooling

BY YEAR OF BIRTH

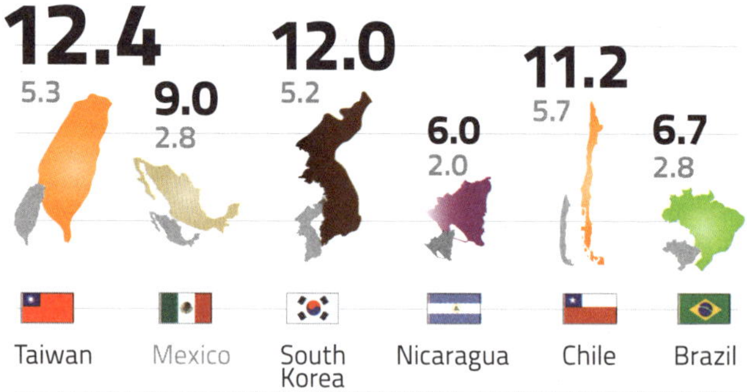

Source: Behrman, Duryea y Székely (1999).

■ 1970
■ 1930

Now, although Mexico has achieved substantial advancements in terms of school enrollment, it is nevertheless lagging behind other countries and, more importantly, it is failing to meet the country's needs. It is entirely clear that Mexico's education system is far from adequate. As various evaluations prove, it is far from meeting the educational needs of families and far from sufficient to accelerate national economic growth.

Nonetheless, the quantity and quality of education received today is far higher than in previous generations. Perhaps this is the reason why most parents do not consider the level of education their children receive to be bad, since they are using their own experience as a reference point.[12]

Another sign of Mexico's transition to a predominantly middle-class society is the participation of women in the workforce. Mexico is transforming into a middle-income country thanks, in part, to women's contributions to household earnings. The following graphs show how women's employment and access to work have changed: although their proportion in the Mexican workforce is still smaller than in some other countries, the number of women working outside the home doubled between the 1980s and 1990s.

More Women in the Labor Force

RATE OF FEMALE PARTICIPATION IN MEXICO'S WORKFORCE (AGES 15-64)

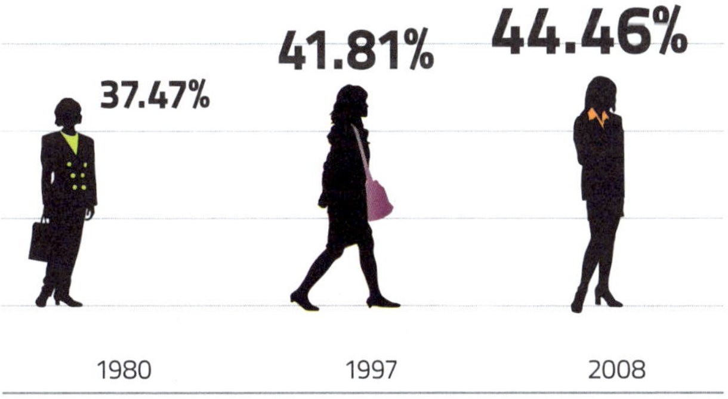

Source: International Labour Organization.

[12] See, for example, the May 2008 survey by the newspaper *Reforma*.

Female Labor Force Participation Rate

PERCENT INCREASE, 1980-2008

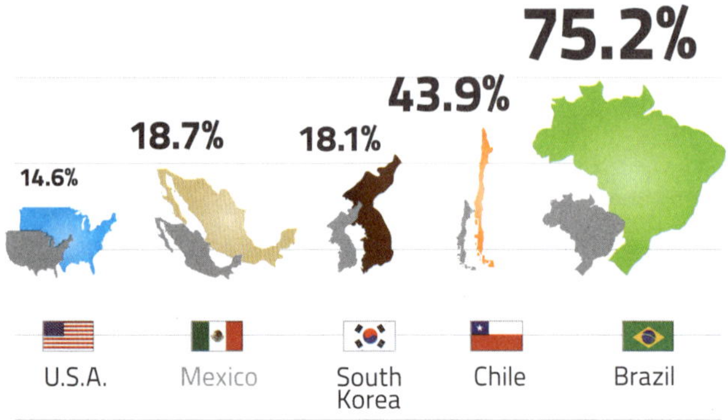

Source: International Labour Organization.

The increase in participation of women in the workforce can be observed in other ways, too: first, in the similarities in labor force participation between men and women today, versus what could be observed 13 years ago.

Workforce Participation by Gender and Age

FOR MEN AND WOMEN IN MEXICO

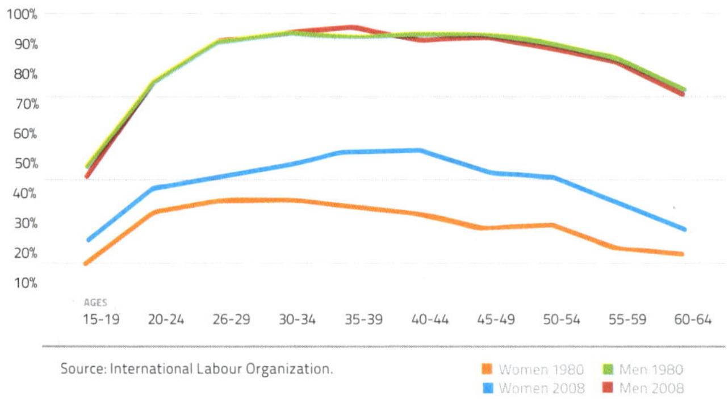

Source: International Labour Organization.

Labor Force Participation of Men and Women in Mexico

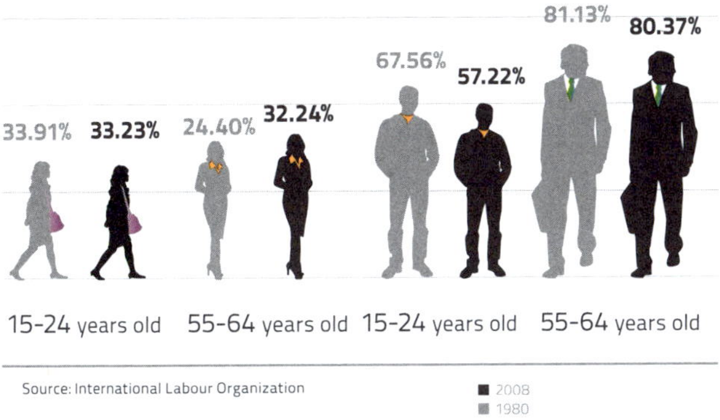

Source: International Labour Organization

And second, in the extent to which increased schooling is linked to greater workforce participation.

Perhaps the most powerful point here is that Mexico has been experiencing these positive trends for years, if not decades. All of the indicators show significant improvements. That is to say that, despite ups and downs, the foundations of a middle class society have been built. Some public policies and events, such as economic crises, have slowed the pace of progress, but they have not undone it. Viewed over an extended period, the overall improvement is significant and the implications are enormous.

From a structurally poor society to a population capable of transforming its way of life

The following graph summarizes what has taken place in Mexico in recent decades: it went from being a relatively poor society to one with consistently improving indicators, starting with those that have the capacity to improve lifestyle and life expectancy. These phenomena are not occurring by coincidence: they represent the result of a steady advance in the factors that make possible the consolidation of a modern, middle-class society.

Economic Indicators Vs. Average Age of Population

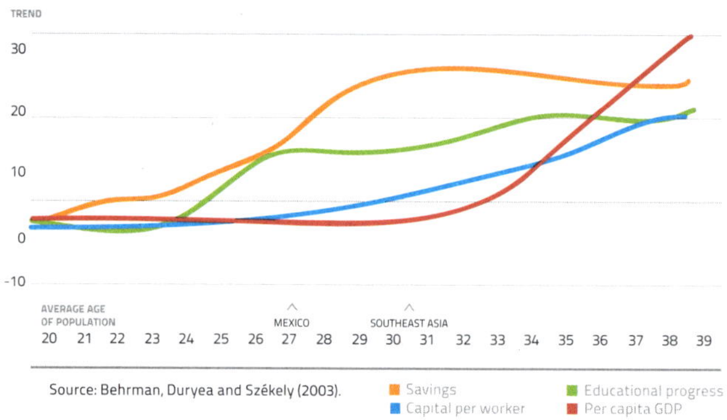

Source: Behrman, Duryea and Székely (2003).

The Mexican population looks more and more like the populations of developed economies, or, at least, it is getting there, even if too slowly. There are many ways to objectively observe the ways in which Mexican society has changed and progressed.

2.2 Consumption patterns of Mexico's middle class

The data provided in previous sections show Mexico's overall advancement in becoming a middle-class society. This means that the basic needs of nearly the majority of the population are being met, and that they can begin consuming more sophisticated products and services and investing in the future.

At the same time, these new necessities imply new problems and therefore, a new wave of public policies to resolve more complex issues such as health, economic stability, credit coverage, etc. Perhaps more than any other type of indicator, the growth of the middle class can be observed in the behavior of the population: to the extent that salaries increase and prices decrease (thanks to controlled inflation levels and greater competition due to imports), the consumption of goods and services that were previously unobtainable rises. Protein consumption, for example, has been rising, showing Mexicans increasingly have sufficient income to allow additional pleasures.

Meat consumption per capita rose by 82%, from 34 kilograms per person in 1990 to 62 in 2005. Not long ago, it would have been unthinkable for the majority of Mexicans to eat meat regularly, and it was common to worry about the available supply and variety of dairy products. In the 1980s, the government painted on buildings the saying, "si la leche es poca, al niño le toca" (roughly translated as "when milk is low, to the little child it goes"). The intention was to educate the population and thus prevent infant malnutrition. In today's Mexico, this message would seem strange and anachronistic.

The increase in the consumption of meat and other products is not only due to higher income per capita but also because they have become more affordable as a result of trade liberalization, increased competition, and significant productivity improvements in production, distribution and marketing.

Increase in Meat Consumption

KILOGRAMS/PERSON/YEAR

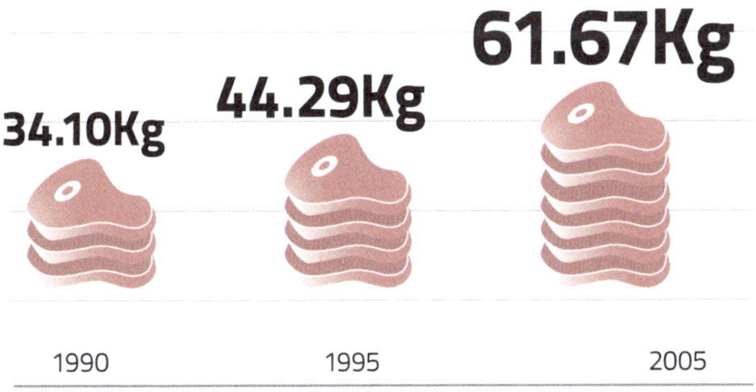

Source: SAGARPA (Secretary of Agriculture, Ranching, Rural Development, Fisheries and Food Supply).

It is interesting to note that during the same period, livestock production in the country expanded significantly, growing from a little over three million tons in 1993 to 5.5 million in 2008.

Decline in the Price of Meat
(INDEX)*

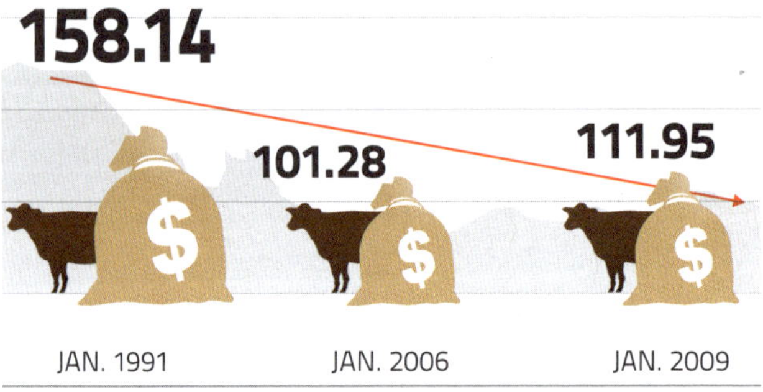

*Coefficient of the consumer price index for meat products (SP528) and the INPC (SP1) (SP1, 2nd half of June 2002=100; SP528 1990=100)

Unfortunately, these changes in consumption patterns are not without a downside. In these same years, the country has gone from being a society with malnutrition in the average population to one in which obesity has become a serious public health concern. Interestingly, the federal government now seeks to prohibit the consumption of junk food in schools, indicating that students destine financial resources to this type of expenditure and that obesity is a top health concern.[13]

Changes in consumption patterns have transformed Mexico from a society with malnutrition to one with obesity

[13] This also suggests that Mexico prefers prohibition to citizen responsibility as public policy, the speed-bump to the stop sign. In this context, it is worth asking whether the middle class is more teachable, more open to civic responsibility.

Although some of these statistics show worrisome patterns, such as those relating to obesity and its health implications, they also illustrate the fact that Mexican society is beginning to resemble the developed world. The same applies to the epidemiological transition in which chronic diseases (hypertension, diabetes, cancers) displace infectious diseases as the primary cause of death and suffering within a society.

The National Survey of Health and Nutrition 2006 confirmed that being overweight is a widespread and growing phenomenon among Mexicans. A quarter of children aged five to eleven years old, one in three teens and nearly seven in ten people over the age of 20 years of age are overweight or obese. Among each of these segments of the population, the number of overweight or obese people was higher in 2006 than in 1999. In fact, Mexico is already the OECD country with the second highest rate of obesity among adults (surpassed only by the United States).

Percent of the Adult Population with Obesity

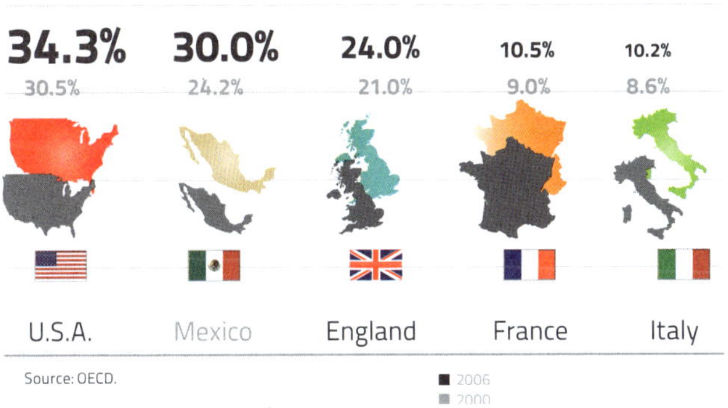

Source: OECD.

Along the same lines, diseases associated with obesity have increased as causes of death in Mexico. According to data from the National Health Information System, diabetes mellitus and heart disease were the two leading causes of death in hospitals in 2005. The increasing prevalence of these diseases as well as the pattern of health spending in Mexico each show an increasing resemblance to that of middle-income societies, where most of the population is middle class. In such a case it becomes necessary to have an advanced health care system that can prevent and resolve problems derived from a change in the consumption patterns of a large portion of the population.

This pattern is also observed in the nascent but important increase in the purchase of private insurance and health plans. Due to the lack of a public health system that works for everyone, insurance plans are purchased to improve the quality of treatment. The acquisition of these services confirms the availability of additional resources in families that can spend to minimize future risks rather than only to address pressing immediate needs. The data shows that public, private, and out-of-pocket health spending has more than doubled in the last 18 years. The increase in private and out-of-pocket spending reflects an improvement in the spending capacity of individuals.

One of the main advantages of *ex ante* private expenditure, or insurance premiums, is the control that it gives families over the costs of unpredictable yet common incidents.

Private Health Spending

MILLIONS OF CONSTANT 2000 PESOS

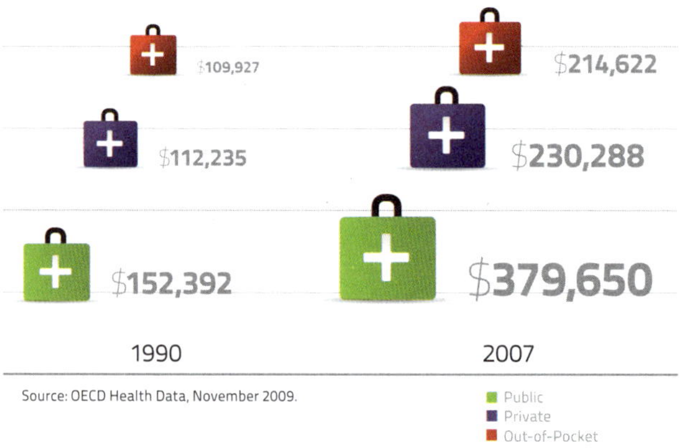

Source: OECD Health Data, November 2009.

Data shows that public, private, and out-of-pocket health spending has more than doubled in the last 18 years

In 2006, 3.7 percent of households in Mexico incurred catastrophic health expenditures: expenses that seriously disrupt family income that are by nature *ex post*.[14] Out-of-pocket spending also tends to be regressive, meaning it disproportionately affects poor and middle class families. By contrast, when an individual or a family has the capacity to dedicate resources to meeting their natural aversion to risk, the increase in wellbeing and peace of mind provided by insurance naturally outweighs the cost of being insured.

Exactly the same behavioral pattern that is seen in private health spending is also evident in the sale of life insurance, whose growth is outpacing that of the overall economy.

Insurance premiums are increasing, creating new sources of savings that, through the financial system, can become sources of financing for economic activity.

Housing is another category in which considerable advances have been made. A growing portion of the population has its own home, a family's primary asset. In the last ten years, seven million units of housing have been built—equivalent to approximately 25% of all homes reported in the 2008 Income-Expenditure Household Survey (26.7 million homes in total were reported). A proper home, whether owned or rented, brings with it additional changes: nuclear families tend to develop their own lifestyle patterns, distinct from families in which various generations live under the same roof.

[14] Secretaría de Salud, Government of Mexico, Comunicado de Prensa No. 434, December 14, 2009.

Value of Insurance Premiums

MILLIONS OF DOLLARS

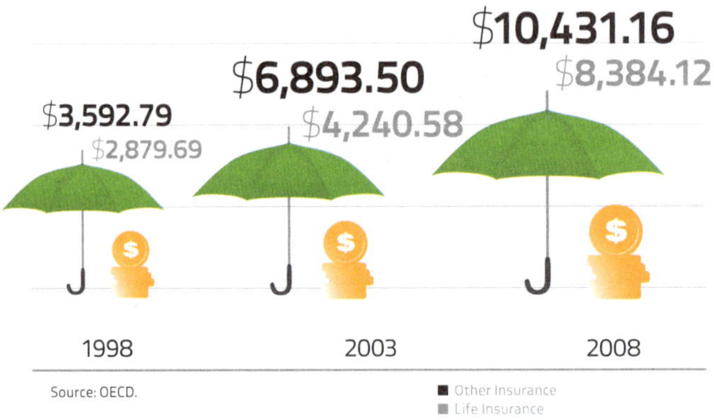

Source: OECD.

Housing has improved in both in size and the inclusion basic services, though without doubt there is much room for improvement. In 1960, 80% of homes had two or fewer rooms and only 20% had basic sanitation facilities. In 2010, 60% of homes have three or more rooms, and 90% have lavatories. Another interesting phenomenon is the increase in government-subsidized housing used as a family's second home: some are rented out, while others are used for weekend getaways. It is estimated that in the states of Morelos and Guerrero, approximately one-third of subsidized housing consists of second homes used for weekends, holidays and vacations.

An ever-greater portion of Mexicans have their own house

Change in Home Sizes

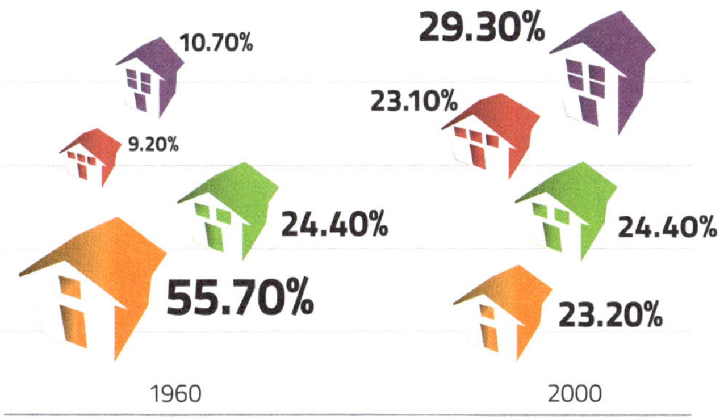

Source: INEGI (National Institute of Statistics and Geography)

with four or more rooms
with three rooms
with two rooms
with one room

The quality of housing has improved; today 60% of homes have three or more rooms

More Homes Have Basic Services

PERCENTAGE OF HOMES WITH BASIC SERVICES

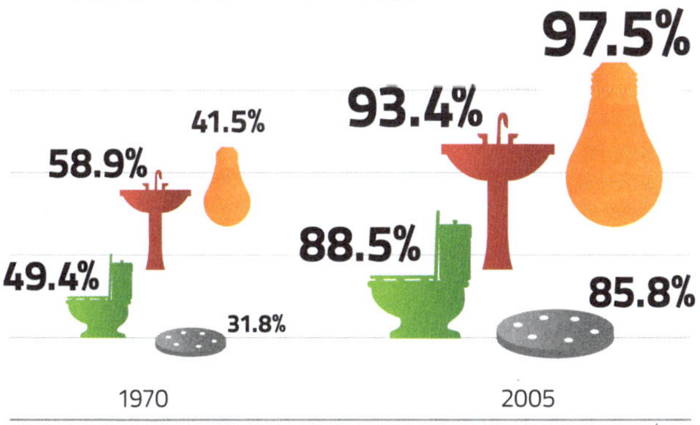

Source: INEGI (National Institute of Statistics and Geography)

Drainage
Running water
Electricity
Lavatory

Increased Home Ownership

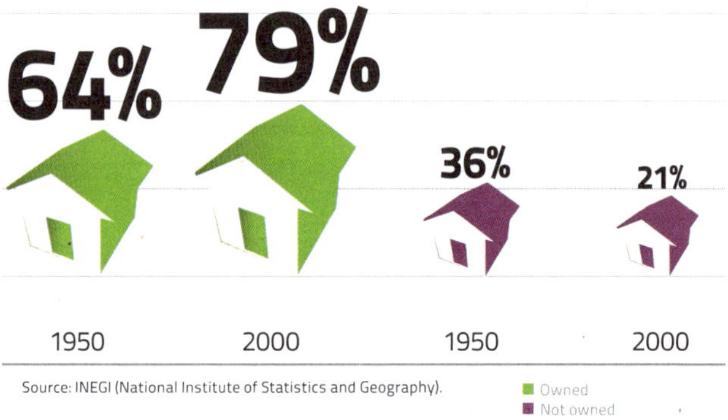

Source: INEGI (National Institute of Statistics and Geography).

One of the images characteristic of Mexico is that of plastic soda bottles protecting the steel rods, or re-bar, sticking up out of the corners of the roofs of many modest homes. These rods, facing the sky, have two explanations related to the theme of this book: on the one hand, they reflect a desire to build a second story; on the other, they are evidence of the inability to construct that second story because of flaws in the financial system and/or problems with land tenancy. A family that leaves re-bar waiting for the construction of a second story has hopes of improving their home and is often predisposed to reconsider their political preferences. That is, they will vote for those who seem to ensure continuity in economic growth and the kind of policies that support this growth, rather than those who propose radical change and thus might bring with them a higher economic risk. Such was the case in 2006, when López Obrador -then mayor of Mexico City- was constructing a second-story to the city's beltway, using this to promote his presidential bid. Perhaps many undecided voters were more interested in the chance to build their own second stories. Across Mexico, everyday one sees fewer steel rods with plastic bottles and more two-story homes—indicative of the increasing availability of resources and credit, which, in turn, are a sign of the growing middle class.

The numbers shown in the preceding pages lead one to ask how the expansion of the middle class has been possible. There are many explanations, but one is

Increased Housing Credit

2003 PESOS

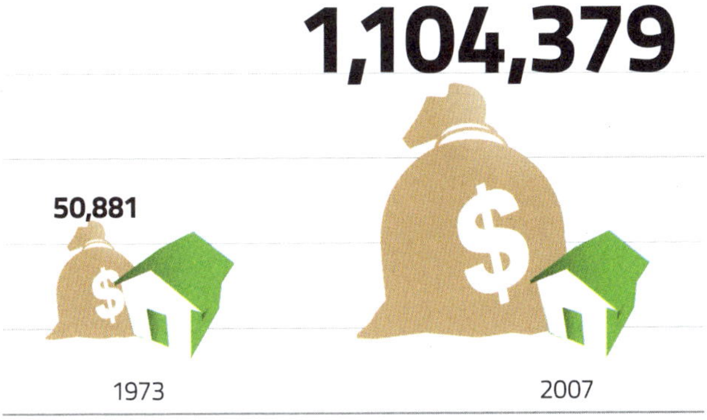

Source: CONAVI (National Housing Commission).

the absence of wealth destruction thanks to macroeconomic stability, in addition to both the availability of credit and an its improved use in recent decades.

Credit hasn't just increased in availability—some of the obstacles that kept it from flowing have been removed. The procedural costs for obtaining credit have been reduced, and advances have been made in resolving legal problems in providing banks and other lending institutions with better guarantees.

The housing program implemented by the federal government since 2000 consisted primarily of identifying those elements that impeded construction, acquisition and home mortgages for the members of the growing middle class. With this practical approach, the government was able to create a housing program that resulted in increased assets for millions of Mexicans, putting in place a platform for the consolidation of the middle class. In doing so, the Mexican government did no more than adopt the developed world's vision that the middle class is key to stability and that its consolidation depends on the ability of a household to accumulate wealth.

In addition, it is worth mentioning how important access to credit has been to Mexicans' ability to purchase automobiles and acquire credit cards.

Registered motor vehicles in circulation in Mexico

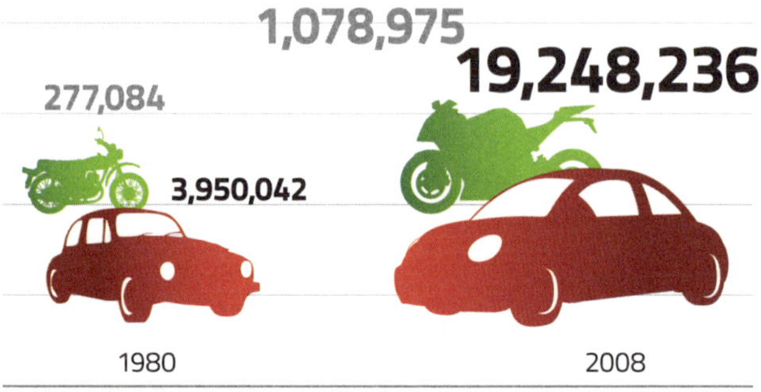

Source: INEGI (National Institute of Statistics and Geography).

Access to credit has increased the capacity to acquire motor vehicles

Credit Cards in Use

AT THE END OF THE QUARTER

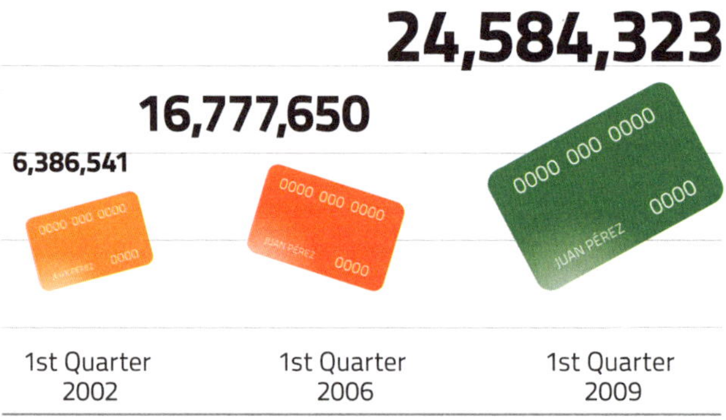

Source: Banco de México (Central Bank)

Of course, credit is a double-edged sword because it operates under the assumption that a person's or a family's income will continually rise so that he can make future payments. For credit to work properly, a culture of repayment is necessary—something not easily achieved in an economy that has been through recurrent financial crises. As has recently been seen in various economies, especially some European nations, the sustainable growth of credit is necessary for development, but an elevated and sustained level of economic growth is needed for repayment. The lack of a healthy balance of financing and growth comprises one of the greatest risks not just to the middle class, but to the stability of an entire country.

THE REACH OF BANKING SERVICES IN MEXICO

The financial system is a basic structure in a country's economy. Financial services include banking, insurance, securities, factoring, capital leasing and capital markets. The accessibility of banking services is a fundamental condition for the development of a financial system.

In particular, the accessibility of banking is essential for the middle class's participation in the financial system, including both investments and loans. The expansion of banking thus becomes the engine of development.

In the case of Mexico, the development of banking services for the middle-class has shown growth but also encountered serious obstacles. Since 2004, the number of users of financial services has doubled, according to the Secretariat of Finance and Public Credit (SHCP). [15] In "The Use of Financial Services in Mexico," the SHCP indicates that approximately 57% of the population has access to the financial system. The number of users from the C segment rose from 63% to 74% in 2007 and 2008 and from 41% to 61% for those in D+. The reasons for this increase in banking accessibility are centered around: a 7% growth in point-of-sales terminals (in 2008 there were 446,000 terminals) for commercial transactions, electronic payroll payments, and an increase in the use of debit cards (24% higher in 2008 than in 2007). Specifically, the use of debit cards has grown due to the installation of the infrastructure to accept card payments in gas stations.

However, access to banking services has still not reached sufficient levels. For exam-

[15] See Box 1 on page 7 for a description of the letter-denominated social strata.

ple, 25% of Mexico's population have no access to bank branches—which implies high transaction costs for the payment of public services, sending remittances, and cashing checks, including those from government transfers like Oportunidades.

Written in collaboration with Rafael Ch.

Another of the more visible phenomena related to the expansion of the middle class is the growing presence of retail stores across the country. Although a measurement of this kind of business in square meters per inhabitant in Mexico reveals a lesser penetration than in developed economies, there has nevertheless been spectacular growth of such stores in Mexico in recent years. According to the economic census, the number of units of department stores, auto repair shops and convenience stores grew 44% between 1998 and 2008 (from 17,321 to 24,942). The rate of expansion has continued despite the economic crisis, which is indicative of the positive expectations of companies dedicated to retail sales to the middle class.

The growing penetration of retail stores points not only to the increasing purchasing power of an important segment of the population, but also to changing lifestyles and consumption patterns. The growth of these businesses signifies a greater availability of basic consumer goods, improved quality, competitive

Growth in Retail Store Floorspace

IN THOUSANDS OF SQUARE METERS

Source: ANTAD (National Association of Department Stores and Auto Repair Shops).

prices, and increases in both the use of electronic forms of payment and in the penetration of the financial system. The growth of retail stores across the country shows that the broad participation of the middle class is not just taking place in the most important cities, but also in the great majority of urban areas. This growth also appears to contradict the constant complaint of many businesspeople that there is no domestic market.

Greater purchasing power and changes in lifestyle and consumption

2.3 Beyond basic needs: entertainment and leisure

It is interesting to observe how, upon obtaining its own home, the behavior patterns of a family, in all categories, begin to change. The growth of the entertainment industry, as evidenced by the number of entertainment establishments, shows the development of businesses that cater to families who can now afford to spend money on more than just the basics. The same can be said for the increase in movie theaters, the use of cell phones and the

Greater Supply of Entertainment

NUMBER OF PUBLIC ENTERTAINMENT ESTABLISHMENTS

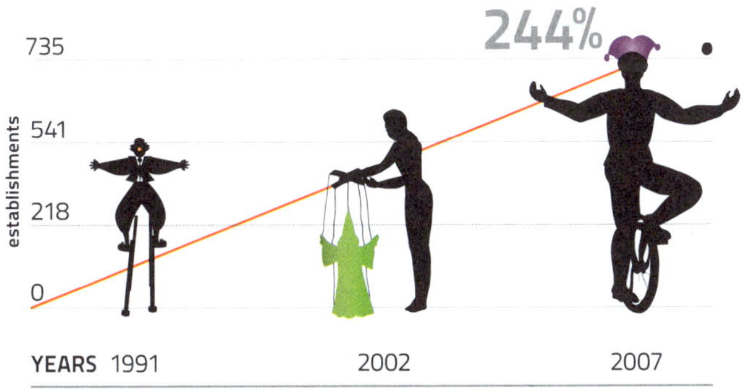

Source: INEGI (National Institute of Statistics and Geography).

Internet, paid television, travel (65% percent of Mexicans travel beyond their own cities at least once a year), the number of passports issued, and many other examples.

In conclusion, as was pointed out at the beginning of the chapter, Mexico

Movie Showings at Mexican Theaters

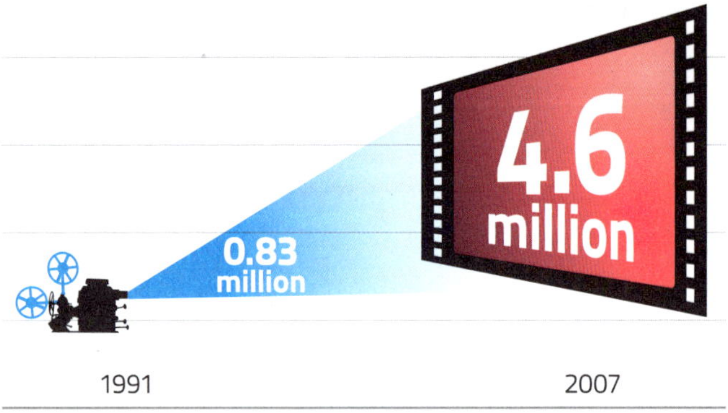

Note: Graph depicts only data that has been reported by establishments.
Source: INEGI (National Institute of Statistics and Geography).

More People Have Internet Access

MILLIONS OF HOME INTERNET USERS IN MEXICO

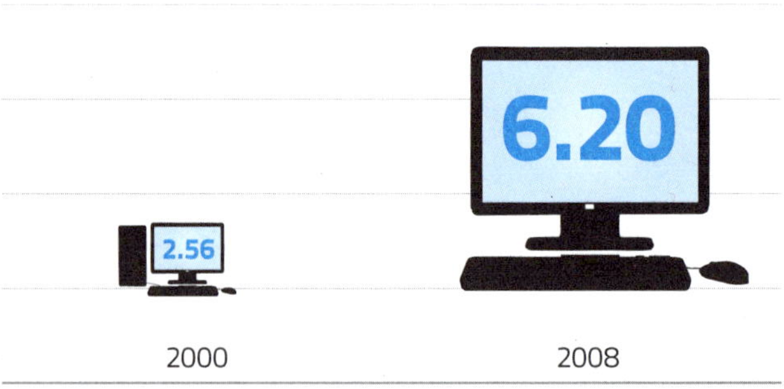

Source: COFETEL (Federal Telecommunications Commission) .

More Mobile Phones, Less Land Lines

TELEPHONE DENSITY

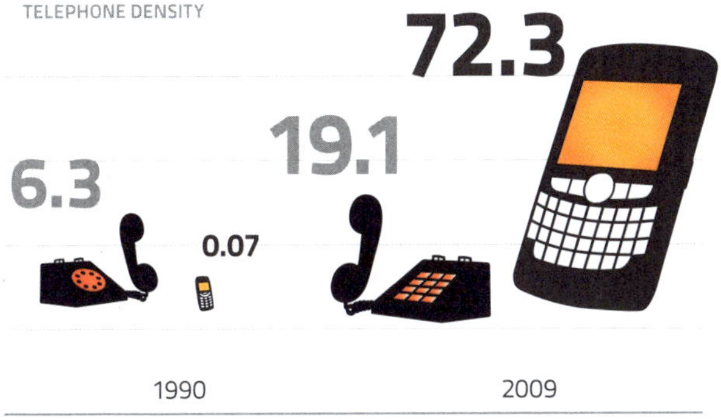

Source: COFETEL (Federal Telecommunications Commission).

■ Mobile phones (number of users per 100 inhabitants)
■ Land lines (number of lines per 100 inhabitants)

The use of cellular telephones and the Internet has grown over the past decade

Paid Television Subscriptions

(SUBSCRIBERS PER THOUSAND INHABITANTS)

Source: Directory of Statistical Market Information COFETEL (Federal Telecommunications Commission), with information from authorized dealers (preliminary data).

Passengers on Mexican Domestic Flights

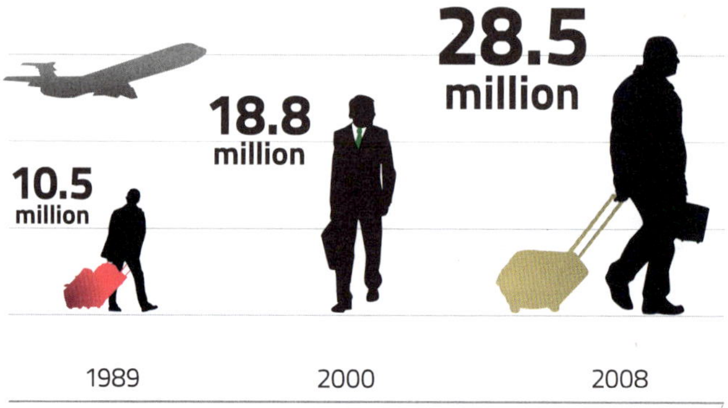

Source: Sectur (Secretary of Tourism).

Today, 65% of Mexicans travel outside of their city at least once a year

More Mexicans Travel Abroad

THOUSANDS OF AIR TRAVELERS

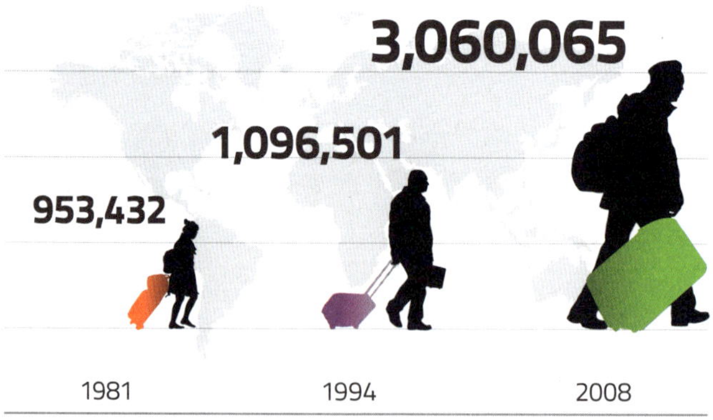

Source: Banco de México (Central Bank)

has experienced an extraordinary transformation, as measured by a variety of indicators. It is difficult for one to appreciate the extent to which things have changed, especially because changes and improvements are typically gradual, accumulating over time. However, if one examines how an urban family in Mexico lived two or three decades ago and compares it to today, the difference is remarkable. Mexican society has experienced a transformation evidenced by its consumption levels, its outlook, and, above all, its perception of the opportunities available for its children. The country has changed, and these indicators give a very good idea of what that change implies in terms of political and economic stability.

* * *

Transformation towards a middle class society

- The increase in GDP per capita translates into an improved quality of life and life expectancy for Mexicans.
- Although widespread poverty exists, Mexico is no longer a poor country.
- The 2006 presidential election caused a spike in in-kind transfers to the lower income population, potentially distorting poverty statistics.
- The existence of more working age people than dependents is conducive to development and the accumulation of wealth.
- Today, Mexicans receive more and better education than their parents.
- From a structurally poor society to a population capable of transforming its quality of life
- Changes in consumption patterns have transformed Mexico from a society challenged by malnourishment to one facing problems of obesity.
- Total health spending—including public, private and out-of-pocket costs—has tripled in 18 years.
- An ever-growing portion of Mexicans own their own home.
- The quality of housing has improved; today 60% of Mexicans live in homes with three or more bedrooms.
- Access to credit has increased the capacity of Mexicans to purchase automobiles.

- Purchasing power has increased, changing lifestyles and patterns of consumption.
- The use of cellular telephones and the Internet has grown in the last decade.
- Today, 65% of Mexicans travel outside their city at least once a year.

The importance of social mobility in strengthening the middle class

Chapter 3

As has been discussed throughout this book, the term "middle class" tends to be associated not just with a combination of consumption preferences and income levels, but also with an outlook that incorporates expectations of improved wellbeing and an inclination to invest time and money into achieving such things.

There is perhaps no concept more important in the development of the middle class than social mobility. A society whose economy promotes professional advancement, the creation of new businesses, and the material improvement of families is a society whose citizens make their way up the social ladder.

Social mobility is nothing other than the movement of people towards improved economic positions during the course of their productive lives. Mobility is linked to personal income growth, and as has been shown here, the income that is most relevant to Mexico's budding middle class is family income. But above all, social mobility is associated with the expectation of systematic improvement. Without such an expectation, there is no reason to invest in development and the essence of a sense of belonging to the middle class is lost. Thus, the possibility of social mobility is a product of the efforts of individuals and families, but can also occur as a result of a government fiscal strategy aimed at redistributing wealth. In both cases, the general economic situation of the country is improved as a result.

It is important to understand that the social mobility achieved during Mexico's era of "stabilizing development"[16] in the 1950s and 1960s was attained through a systematic increase in the nation's productivity. In that time, three factors combined to enable such conditions: a) financial stability (low inflation, prudent management of economic policy, very few burdensome regulations, and a stable and predictable exchange rate); b) a consistently clear direction with respect to the objectives of economic policy and the function of both government and private companies; and, c) a rather uncomplicated and uncompetitive domestic and international environment. These three elements facilitated economic growth development of businesses and individuals, all of which translated into high rates of productivity growth, which is, in the end, the fundamental factor that explains social mobility. In the 1950s and '60s, the demographic pressure was also less than in the 1980s and '90s, as there were fewer dependents (minors and retirees) per working-age person.

[16] During the 1950s and 60s, the country's GDP grew at rates of over 6%.

The economic crises that followed undermined social mobility as much as they did the growth in productivity that had been achieved. Even worse were the government's responses to the crises, which created permanent obstacles to investment, people's development, and the efficient workings of the economy. If indeed the past 15 years have favored economic stability, there is nevertheless much advancement to be made toward creating the conditions that favor sustainable economic growth.

3.1 Inequality of income and opportunity

Historically, Mexico has experienced normal processes of mobility within society, but its economic performance in recent years has been insufficient to give it a decisive boost. At the same time, Mexico has countless impediments and obstacles to social mobility.

For centuries, poverty has coexisted alongside wealth in a way that sharpens tensions in Mexican society—above all, because of the expectations the situation generates. This rift persists, and in some cases is widened by structural changes, technology, and the development of the knowledge economy.

The growth of the middle class has occurred alongside a modest improvement in social inequality indices. According to the Gini index, a coefficient of one means wealth is highly concentrated within a narrow segment, while

Despite greater social mobility, a significant gap exists between the rich and the poor

Total Nominal Income

QUARTERY, 2008

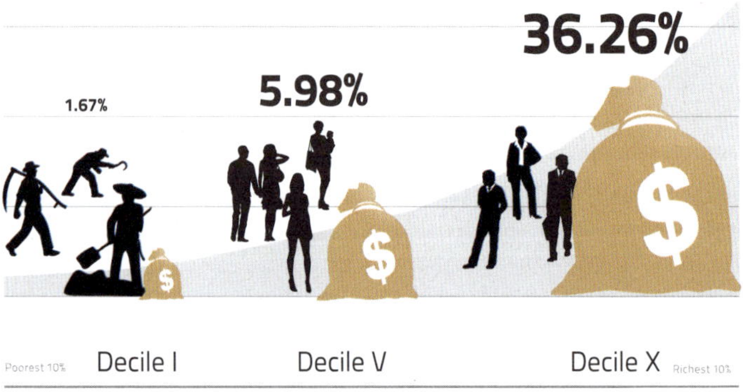

*Each decile represents one-tenth of all the data collected
Source: Created by the authors using data from ENIGH, the National Household Income and Expenditure Survey.

a coefficient of zero means income is equally distributed. Of course, no society reaches either extreme. However, what's important is for the coefficient to be shrinking—in other words, that the coefficient be trending toward zero.

Inequality in Mexico

GINI COEFFICIENT

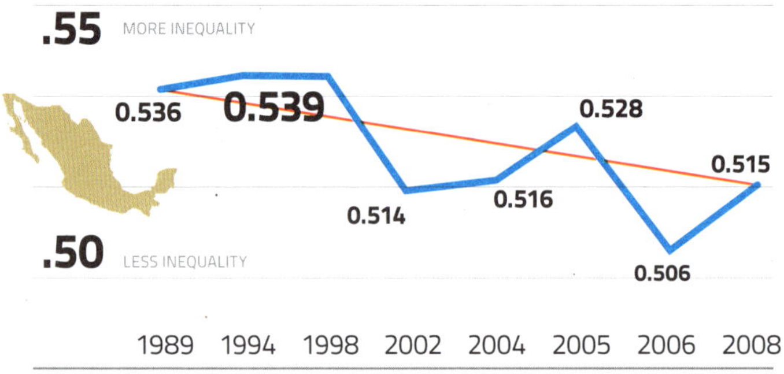

Source: Economic Commission for Latin America and the Caribbean.

Inequality in itself does not limit social mobility, although it is the result of a lack of access (or, in other words, human capital), especially to education and the Internet, which are necessary for individual economic progress. According to the ESRU (Espinosa Rugarcía Foundation) 2006 Social Mobility Survey, Mexico is a country with little social mobility, especially at the extremes. Radical movements—in other words, those from the poorest quintile (one-fifth) of the population to the wealthiest fifth, and vice versa—are extremely rare. At medium income levels, the situation is more hopeful. 17% of people whose parents were part of the third quintile and 13% of people whose parents were part of the fourth quintile were able to rise to the wealthiest quintile of the Mexican population.

ASPIRATIONS REFLECTED IN FOREIGN NAMES

In their aspirations for social mobility, Mexicans are increasingly likely to give their children foreign names. The National Register of the Population publishes information regarding the most popular Mexican names, based on birth certificates registered in the country. In the 2008 list of 50 most popular baby names, for example, is a noticeable selection of such aspirational names, many of them in other languages, particularly English. Among them are Vanessa (#18), Elizabeth (#24), Evelyn (#28), Abigail (# 30), Monserrat (#33), Lizbeth (#37), Ana Karen (#38), Marely (#47), Jacquelin (#48) and Jacqueline (#49). For men the most popular non-Spanish names are Alexander (15th), Jonathan (29th), Alexis (32nd), Kevin (35th), Cristian (36th), Brayan (38th). [17]

This phenomenon is also present in the naming of Mexican schools. Interestingly, a significant proportion of private educational establishments choose foreign names

The yearning for social mobility is reflected in the foreign names given to children and educational institutions

[17] See: http://www.babycenter.com.mx/pregnancy/nombres/nombres_mas_populares_2008_mexico/.

that carry an aspirational quality, in an effort to attract middle-class students. For example, of the 905 private primary and middle schools registered in 2009 in Iztapalapa, a working class neighborhood in Mexico City, 437 either have foreign names or are named after places in foreign countries. It is noteworthy that 17 Iztapalapa schools (all private) are ranked among the top five percent in all of Mexico.[18]

Frequency at which Children Have a Better, Worse, or Similar Level of Economic Well-Being as Their Parents

CHILDREN \ PARENTS	Quintile 1 (Poorest 20%)	Quintile 2	Quintile 3	Quintile 4	Quintile 5 (Richest 20%)
Quintile 5	4%	6%	17%	26%	59%
Quintile4	7%	13%	20%	29%	26%
Quintile 3	15%	26%	26%	25%	12%
Quintile 2	26%	28%	23%	16%	3%
Quintile 1	48%	27%	14%	5%	0%

*Each quintile represents one-fifth of all the collected data.
Source: Social mobility survey, Espinosa Yglesias.

Quintile 1 Quintile 2 Quintile 3 Quintile 4 Quintile 5

It is also important to note that a good proportion of Mexicans perceive greater social mobility than actually exists. Only 11% of people who suffered a precipitous drop in their level of economic wellbeing say they felt it, while 35% of them even perceived an improvement. It should be noted that social mobility is not only reflected in increased revenues, but also in access to new products and services, as well as the ability to invest in the future.

[18] See the webpage, www.comparatuescuela.org

In effect, the results of this survey imply that the middle class perceives (albeit sometimes incorrectly) an imporvement in well-being with respect to the previous generation. This perception reflects the fact that people consider their social and economic position in the long-term, taking into acount short-term fluctuations but rarely re-defining their status based on them.

A good portion of Mexicans perceive greater social mobility than actually exists

3.2 Causes and effects of inequality

There are two dynamics at play that explain Mexico's inequality. One has to do with the absence of equal opportunities. In Mexican society, the child of a family with resources has far more opportunities to progress in life than does the child of a rural farming family living on the verge of poverty. The other dynamic has to do with the way in which the world economy has been transforming, and with the abilities and capacities of every individual within this context.

Unlike differences in the conditions of origin that distinguish individuals, equal opportunity is an essential condition for society's progress. The family one is born into, the place where one lives, and the surrounding conditions are factors that, at least early in life, one cannot choose. In contrast, equal opportunity has to do with the legal framework and public policies that characterize a society. Perhaps the most obvious factors that have historically contributed to equal opportunity are education, health care, and the ability to emigrate. Although they are not the only means available, these vehicles allow some compensation for differences in origin, or at least help to level the playing field.

In today's world, another factor has come into play: having a computer and connectivity—in other words, having Internet access as a way to connect with the rest of the world and learn the most up-to-date information.

Technological development in recent decades has created a new distribution of benefits in almost all countries. The social differences within economies have intensified because what has become most valuable is no longer that which is linked to brute force, but rather what can be achieved through knowledge. If a Chinese person, a Haitian, or a Mexican can perform the exact same industrial process but at different costs, it is because the ability to compete at this level is reduced to three factors: productivity, salary, and transportation costs. Productivity depends on the technology used and on the value added by each company and worker. Thus, with equal technologies and factoring in transportation costs, wages determine who stays in the market and who is forced out.

In the service sector, the differences become much more apparent, opening up countless opportunities. The effort India has put forth to take part in the globalization process by providing services that go far beyond industrial manufacturing is particularly relevant. In value added services (those that require creativity and intellectual capacity), what counts is not the ability to sew a thousand buttons a minute, or to pull a lever a certain way every certain number of seconds, but rather the ability to solve problems and incorporate new ideas. In its most primitive version, such as the call centers for which Bangalore has become famous, workers have to resolve fairly simple problems, such as questions about bank accounts, or how to

Productivity today depends not on one's physical power, but on the technology employed to harness the power of knowledge

fix a computer issue or stereo. As things grow more complex, the services provided include preparing tax returns, readings and interpretations of clinical or radiographic analyses, the design and development of software, *etcetera*.

In the information age, socioeconomic differences are deepened because what matters are the intrinsic capabilities of individuals, which depend largely on two sources: those developed at home and in the family environment, and those provided through the education and health systems. Some of these differences are inevitable: an urban and a rural child may be born with the same attributes and into identical families, but the urban setting provides a stimulus far more powerful than the rural (Internet access and a good transportation system can close this gap). Other differences are not the result of the environment but rather of public policy: knowledge, health and skills development are factors that are derived directly from the health and educational systems. In India, a country infinitely more complex than Mexico, there has been remarkable progress in education that explains the country's success, even if small for a nation-continent so vast.

Although there are many reasons why social and regional differences exist (between northern and southern Mexico, for example), one of the most significant is infrastructure. There is no doubt that southern Mexico is far more disconnected from the rest of the world than northern Mexico. While the country's average level of infrastructure development leaves much to be desired, the regional differences are particularly striking. Such contrasts entail serious consequences for each region's development. A lack of infrastructure favors the existence of caciques and concentrates enormous power in the hands of local and state governments. At the same time, the relative isolation in these areas creates ample opportunity for corruption and monopolies. No less important, this lack of infrastructure translates into government abuses, public insecurity and, above all, an impotency on the part of the citizens to instigate social and economic changes. The point is that Mexico's regional differences in infrastructure enable (in fact, they promote and explain) the struggling state in which much of the country still lives.

According to the Human Capital Survey conducted by CIDAC (the Center of Research for Development), families with a collective income of less than ten thousand pesos per month have little access to the Internet and a low probability of their children learning English and computer skills. Although these can be compensated to some extent by public libraries and other ways of accessing the Internet, there is no doubt that in the digital age, in which knowledge is a determining factor in a person's income level, Internet access is key. Social mobility in today's world corresponds directly with this phenomenon.

Beyond birthplace, many other factors influence social mobility. An obvious one is education. If access to a primary school education is key to achieving equal opportunity, the level of schooling one achieves in his life will be key to determine his or her social mobility. A person who finishes university has a greater probability of climbing the social ladder than one who only finished primary school.

The evidence in Mexico points to education having an enormous impact on one's income. As can be seen in the following graph, the labor market pays people with a college degree substantially more than it will pay someone without one. Although access to education in Mexico improved considerably during the 20th century (nearly reaching universal access to primary and secondary schooling), important inequalities in access to educational opportunities and education quality persist at all levels. There is still not sufficient access to high school education, much less the quality demanded by the knowledge economy, international competition and social necessities.

Internet access and education are key to social mobility

Salary by Level of Schooling Completed

MOVING AVERAGE, REAL JUNE 2008 PESOS

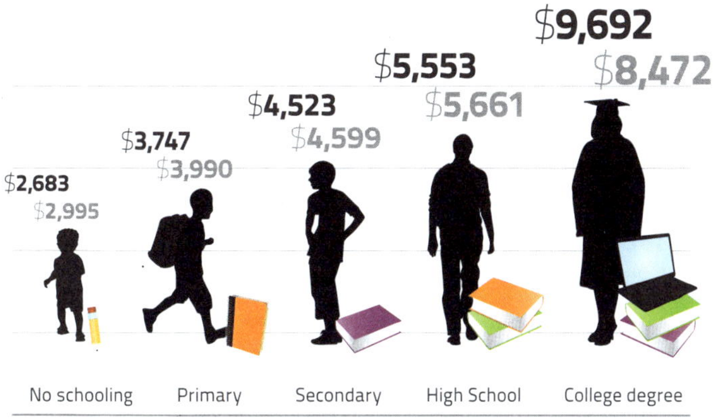

Source: Created using data from surveys by ENEU (National Urban Employment Survey), ENE (National Employment Survey), and the ENOE (National Occupation and Employment Survey) by INEGI (National Institute of Statistics and Geography)

THE MIDDLE CLASSES GO TO COLLEGE

Several decades ago, a college education was a dream few could access. In 1950, just one in every hundred college-aged people was enrolled in university courses.

In contrast, today 27 of every 100 college-aged students are getting a higher education. Though still less than other countries with similar levels of development, the improvement is significant. The change is due in large part to the middle classes making their way into university classes.

Today, 40% of the college-age, middle-income population makes up 32% of enrollment in higher education (while the poorest make up just 8% of enrollment).

If a college-age person lives in a city and comes from a middle- or high-income family, the probability that he is enrolled in an institute of higher education is 45%.

For middle-class families in Mexico, sending their children to university is a feasible goal, though it does require varying levels of effort and sacrifice. It is a goal that, like owning a home or an automobile, represents one of the defining qualities of belonging to the middle class.

For the very poorest sectors of society, a university degree is central to their aspirations of social mobility. Despite the difficulties of access, at the beginning of this decade half of the students receiving higher education were the first generation from their families with access to this level educational level.

More than a symbol of prosperity, a university degree is associated with economic advancement. Despite what is said about the crisis in professional employment, in Mexico there is an income reward for higher education. In 2007, a professional worker earned an average of 74% more than a person who attended only high school.

In this sense, the expansion of the middle class and university enrollment feed off one another. Furthermore, the two depend on common factors: growth in the population's real income, the modernization of the economy, smaller-sized families, and the influence the urban middle class has had on public policy in Mexico.

References

1 Rubio Oca, Julio (ed.), *La política educativa y la educación superior en México. 1995-2006: Un Balance*, Secretariat of Public Education, Cultural Economic Fund, Mexico 2006.

2 Katja Maria Kaufmann, "Understanding the Income Gradient in College Attendance in Mexico: The Role of Heterogeneity in Expected Returns to College," Stanford Institute for Economic Policy Research, 2008.

3 Julio Rubio, *op. cit.*

4 De Garay Sánchez, Adrián, "Los actores desconocidos, una aproximación al conocimiento de los estudiantes," ANUIES, 2001.

5 Estrada, Ricardo, "Ingreso Laboral de los Profesionistas en México por área del conocimiento 1988-2007," CIDAC working paper, available at www.cidac.org.

Written in collaboration with Ricardo Estrada

Education opens new horizons. It facilitates the understanding of different cultures, communication via the Internet, travel, and the adaptation and comprehension of different codes of conduct. An extreme example can be seen in the Mexicans who migrate to the United States. Exposed to an open labor market and a better environment for growth, migrants continuously find ways to adapt and prosper. In Mexico, there are still significant gaps in skills that prevent the country from increasing its competitiveness vis-à-vis the United States, as illustrated by the graph below.

English and Computer Skills by Level of Family Income

AVERAGES ON THE ENGLISH LANGUAGE INDEX AND COMPUTER SKILLS INDEX

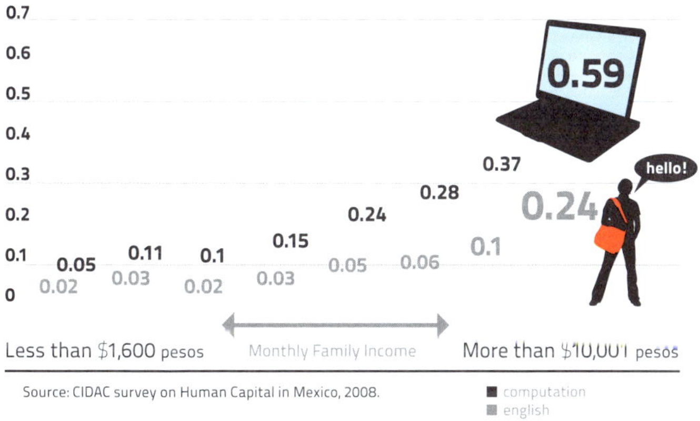

Source: CIDAC survey on Human Capital in Mexico, 2008.

Mexico's insufficient levels of education and skills inhibit social mobility to the extent that they do not produce the conditions necessary for a majority of the population to enter into new, high value-added enterprises.

A lack of sufficient education and skills inhibit social mobility

The informal sector has attractive benefits, yet also great costs

Another indicator influencing the high inequality found in Mexico is the middle classes' association with the informal economy. Informality is a phenomenon that occurs when an economy parallel to the formal economy exists—one that doesn't pay taxes or comply with relevant regulations. Researchers on the subject know that there are many circumstances that lead to informality, but without doubt the greatest of those is the cost of joining the formal economy. In Mexico, there are also a combination of incentives for informality, such as Seguro Popular (a free government insurance plan providing medical services to those not enrolled in the traditional plans associated with the formal sector) and scholarships awarded to those with low family incomes[19].

It is no coincidence that the many requirements and costs involved in complying with the rules of the formal economy drive many producers and merchants to the informal sector. This world has enormous appeal, but also great costs. The principal benefit of joining the informal economy is fact that the obstacles to doing one's daily work are fewer. However, there are also costs: in limits to growth (due to lack of access to bank credit); in the abuses of inspectors, criminals; in the clientelism that inevitably emerges and that primarily affects informal merchants; and, in general, in the scale of operations that makes growth impossible.

A concrete example of this can be seen in the contrast between the rules that govern the development of businesses in Mexico and the United States. As the story goes, "in 2000, when Antonio Villaraigosa was speaker of the California State Assembly, he was dining at the home of the businessman Carlos Slim when he was asked to explain, from his perspective

[19] Those in the informal sector, due to not having formally measurable incomes, are considered to have low incomes, even though this is not always the case.

as a Mexican-American, the difference between the U.S. and Mexico. His answer was: 'It's very simple; if my family had stayed in Mexico I would be serving you this food.' Before the guests confused looks, the current mayor of Los Angeles added: 'Instead, they went to United States and now all of you offer this dinner in my honor.'" Villaraigosa explained that the main reason he had triumphed in the U.S. was because it is a place where the middle class can grow and develop and is fertile ground for the creation of a prosperous and democratic society.[20]

The regulatory framework and incentives of the Mexican economy tend to create obstacles, skew opportunities in favor of a very few, reduce competition, impede the development of new businesses, and limit individual potential. This explains why there is a very important group of large and small businesses, but relatively few medium-sized businesses, that are, in the world in general, the principal sources of innovation and job creation. In other words, although the rhetoric in Mexico focuses on the concept of small and medium businesses, the reality is that in Mexico, there are very few medium-sized businesses and many micro-enterprises.

Finally, one characteristic of Mexico's job market is that much of the hiring done by government entities and private companies has less to do with an applicant's merit and more to do with his personal and family connections. Though this may not be exclusive to Mexico, the lack of competition in some sectors of the economy and the limited development of human capital accentuate this phenomenon in Mexico. Due to the lack of competition,

Regulatory frameworks and incentive structures foment economic development; Mexico lacks these

20 "La clase media mexicana, Carlos J. McCadden M. y Raúl Bravo Aduna. Revista Este País, 213.

businesses and the government itself have very few incentives to improve their capacities. The limited development of human capital means that, without a large stockpile of available talent, personal connections continue to have a greater impact on hiring decisions. Even the labor victories of the unions tend to create privileged, noncompetitive sectors set apart from a relatively poor society. That is to say, a balance between has yet to be found between worker protections on one side and labor and social mobility on the other.

Within this context, worker mobility ends up being the best instrument for guaranteeing labor rights—without it, the employer could further abuse those who lack other employment opportunities. Expanding the range of options for individual workers—in terms of emigration and movement —among job positions, geographic areas and sectors—is the best way to promote development and the consolidation of the middle class (as long as they are willing to take the necessary risks).

On top of all of these factors, one must be added that could be categorized as residual: the sum of the obstacles and sense of dejection generated by the system of biases that limits social mobility. These tend to be reflected in attitudes and behaviors that reinforce the obstacles already in place. Just as merit is given little value in Mexican society, the same is true for anyone who excels: Instead of becoming a model for others, studious children become the target of infantile jokes. Similarly, successful companies are rarely publicly appreciated for their achievements. On the contrary, it will be largely

A balance between protecting workers rights and encouraging social and labor mobility has not been found

Social mobility consolidates the middle class and, at the same time, strengthens the stability and development of the country

assumed that the company relied on access to special favors and privileges in order to achieve its success.

In Mexico, there is a tendency to favor mediocrity, discount success and assume, in the words of an often repeated Mexican saying, that "he who does not cheat will not get ahead."

Social mobility is the key to consolidating the middle class and facilitating the country's long-term stability and development. Despite the relatively benign picture depicted in the statistics of the previous chapter, the apparent paradox between social mobility and stability illustrates the size of the challenge facing Mexico. There is no way to accelerate social mobility without increasing productivity, because this factor lies at the heart of economic growth. A rapidly growing economy generates opportunities for wealth and job creation, as well as better jobs. In short, it creates the conditions for reducing poverty and accelerating social mobility. It is worth repeating the aforementioned paradox: stability is necessary for the kind of change that results in higher productivity and, therefore, progress. That is how many who do not want change end up promoting instability.

Attention should therefore be focused on policies that eliminate obstacles to productivity growth, because this will unleash forces that will strengthen and consolidate Mexico as a middle-class country. Social mobility is a result of public policies that break down barriers and impediments to development.[21] In the case of Mexico, a strategy oriented toward and dedicated to increasing productivity would require prioritizing the elimination of the many obstacles and barriers impeding accelerated economic growth in order to promote a rapid increase in social mobility.

* * *

[21] In this sense, development is freedom, as Amartya Sen has written.

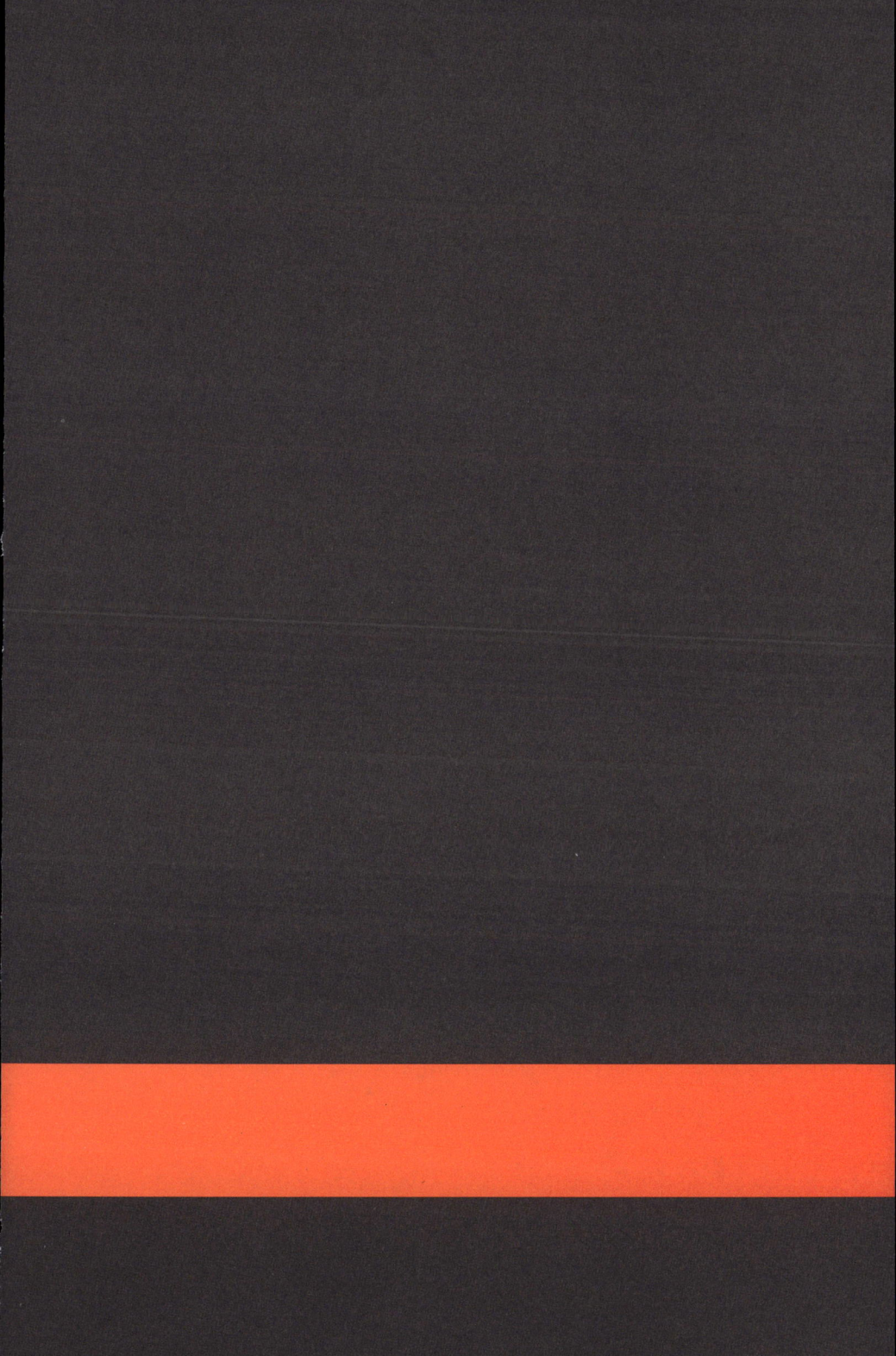

The two central arguments of this book are, first, that Mexico has become a middle-class society that, while still at a precarious stage, has nevertheless been transformed on all fronts, and second, that there is nothing more important to Mexico's future–to its development and stability–than strengthening and expanding its middle class, especially right now, when the global and domestic economic situations have changed growth patterns and dampened expectations about the future. In such circumstances, the pertinent question should be: what makes a society advance toward becoming a middle-class nation, and what can be done to help it advance in that direction?

It is important to recognize that despite appearances and independent of the current global economic crisis, there is no doubt that diverse segments of the Mexican population have experienced substantial economic improvements in recent years (even though the gap between the rich and poor persists). The past 15 years of economic stability and the demographic window have made possible the growth of the middle class–just as happened in the 1950s and '60s. The second chapter of this book shows how this has taken place and why the Mexican process has been distinct, above all because (though this phenomenon is not exclusive to Mexico) the growth of the middle class has more to do with a family's combined income rather than the employment or salary of any one individual.

Mexico's economic stability and the growth of the middle class are due, in essence, to four factors that have been described. First is the drop in fertility rates and the reduction in the dependency ratio–the number of children and elderly dependents over the size of the workforce.

Second is the macroeconomic strategy specifically dedicated to achieving stability; that is, a modest fiscal deficit and monetary policy designed to combat inflation. It is no coincidence that the common denominator between the two great eras of middle-class growth in Mexico (1950s and '60s, and from about 1995 until the present day) has been financial and economic stability, even when rates of economic growth have been less than spectacular.

The third factor is economic openness and the elimination of barriers to investment and commerce. Of course, these measures have not been employed sufficiently to achieve high levels of economic growth, but the important and transcendental role they play in making essential goods and services available to the middle class should not be underestimated. The fourth factor has to do with the significant expansion of education, health care, and poverty reduction programs.

Within this context of economic and social advancement, the greatest challenge the Mexican middle class faces lies in the economic crisis that has affected the world and, with particular severity, the domestic economy. The risk is double: first, families who have already achieved middle-class status could lose their ability to maintain it; second, the general lack of economic growth limits opportunity and social mobility, translating into widespread stagnation and, consequently, fewer possibilities for families to join Mexico's middle class.

The challenge, as has been described, is not just preventing the erosion of the incipient middle class, but is rather creating the conditions that will serve as a platform to support its growth. Such an opportunity could materialize if, as part of government led strategy, the main obstacles to growth were removed. This could serve to not only hasten economic recovery but also to pave the way to greater productivity and social mobility.

In considering how to consolidate the middle class, one must understand the dynamics of the transformation in goods and services production that has taken place, and especially the means of adding value in the current world economy. It means strengthening the factors that have been mentioned: taking advantage of the fleeting demographic window; maintaining macroeconomic stability to avoid recurring crises that destroy wealth; expanding openness and competition in all economic sectors; and revolutionizing the education and health care systems to meet the needs and expectations of the country's citizens.

In this bicentennial year of Mexico's independence, it is worth asking whether the country is reaching maturity at 200 years old. The answer rests in its capacity to become a middle-class country. Conditions in 2010 are far better than in 1810 or 1910, thanks to democracy, albeit imperfect, a more competitive economy, despite burdensome monopolies in some sectors, a demographic window that represents a one-time opportunity for achieving authentic development, and without doubt, a majority middle-class population in spite of many analysts' and politicians' failure to recognize it.

* * *

Bibliography

› Angus, Deaton. *Price Indexes, Inequality, and the Measurement of World Poverty*, American Economic Review 2010, 100:1, 5-34.

› Briceño, Manuel, Jáuregui, D.J., *La Política, Aristóteles, versión directa del original griego*, Panamericana Editorial, 2000, Santafé de Bogotá, p. 188.

› Carlos J. McCadden M. y Raúl Bravo Aduna, *La clase media mexicana*, Revista *Este País*, 213.

› Cooley,Thomas F., *Has Rising Inequality Destroyed The Middle Class? Forbes online*, 2009.

› Court, David y Narasimhan, Laxman, *Capturing the world's emerging middle class*, Mc Kinsey Quarterly, julio 2010.

› Esquivel, Gerardo, *The Dynamics of Income Inequality in Mexico since NAFTA*, El Colegio de México, 2008.

› Méndez, M.L. (2008) *Middle Class Identities in a Neoliberal age: tensions between contested authenticities*, The Sociological Review, Volume 56, Number 2, pp. 220-237.

› Moreno, Alejandro. *La decisión electoral: Votantes, partidos y democracia en México*, Miguel Ángel Porrúa, 2009, México DF.

› Sen, Amartya, *Development as Freedom*, Random House, 1999, New York.

› Szekely, Miguel. *Es posible un México con menor pobreza y desigualdad.* "En México: Crónicas de un País Posible", Fondo de Cultura Económica, 2005.

› Webber, Jude, *Oxford economists draw up system to reveal more detailed picture of poverty*, "Financial Times", julio 2, 2010.

› Wheary, Jennifer (2009). *The Global Middle Class is here: Now What?* World Policy Institute, Winter 2009/10, Vol. 26, No. 4, pp. 75-83.

› *Two billion more bourgeois*, "The Economist" print edition, febrero 12, 2009.

› *Baja 1.6% ingreso de hogares mexicanos*, "El Universal" en línea, julio 16, 2009.

› Secretaría de Salud, Comunicado de Prensa No. 434, diciembre 14, 2009.